W9-BEK-703

Adventures in Phonics

Level A

A publication of
Christian Liberty Press
502 West Euclid Avenue
Arlington Heights, Illinois 60004

Written by Florence M. Lindstrom
Layout and editing by Edward J. Shewan
Copyediting by Belit M. Shewan and Diane Olson
Cover design by Bob Fine

ISBN 1-930092-75-X

Printed in the United States of America

Introduction

The primary goal of phonics instruction is to give each student the ability to decode the proper *sound* for each letter-symbol in the alphabet. Once your student truly understands the basic rules of phonics, along with the appropriate letter sounds, the world of reading will open up to him. Moreover, learning through phonics builds a good speller.

It is important for the teacher to follow the instructions located in the *Adventures in Phonics Level A* Teacher's Manual regarding how and when to use the phonics flashcards and phonics word charts that accompany the student's workbook. These supplemental materials can help your student to grasp the principles of phonics as you systematically drill each important concept presented in the phonics workbook.

This manual also indicates when the *Christian Liberty Phonics Readers* should be introduced. The teacher should first read the introduction to each reader, found on the inside front cover, before the student begins the lessons in the reader. These readers reinforce what he is learning in the *Adventures in Phonics Level A* workbook. Use the following chart as a suggested guideline for beginning the lessons in the four readers:

Workbook Page	Title of Reader
74 or 84	*It is Fun to Read*
100	*Pets and Pals*
122	*A Time at Home*
157	*It is a Joy to Learn*

Each workbook page is perforated so that teachers can easily remove pages if this helps the student in completing his work. All work, however, should be carefully saved for review purposes.

The two most important attributes of a phonics teacher are loving patience and caring perseverance. May the Lord grant you, the instructor, an abundant supply of both.

We express our grateful appreciation for permission to use illustrations from *Thank You, God*, and *We Show Our Love*, © 1963, David C. Cook Publishing Co., Elgin, IL 60120.

Florence Lindstrom

Arlington Heights, Illinois

Page 1

Purpose

To begin to teach the recognition and sound of the short vowel **a.**

Before class begins

1. Remove flashcard **a A** from the set of flashcards.
2. Open to the first page or tear it from the workbook, and set it aside.

Lesson

Eagerly explain that today the student will begin to learn one of the sounds we make as we speak and read. Show the flashcard and say its short vowel *sound*. Have the student repeat the sound three times after you as you point to the three ways it is printed, listening to hear that he makes the correct sound. We can hear this sound in **a**-pple, **a**-x, **a**-nt, **a**-nchor, etc.

Look at the blue box at the top of the page. The top letter **a** is how people print it; the middle letter **A**, or capital letter, is used for proper names, as in Adam and Ann; and the bottom letter **a** is how many computers and word processors print it.

Place the flashcard near the work area so it is seen as the page is being studied.

Follow directions and complete the work.

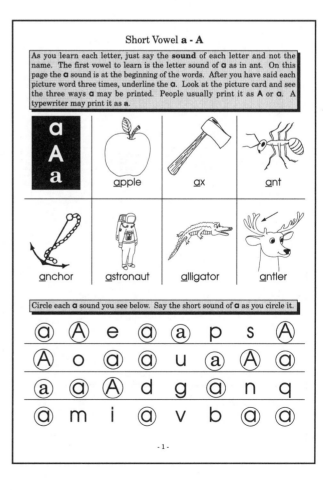

Page 2

Purpose

1. To continue to teach the recognition and sound of the short vowel **a**.

2. To teach the proper formation of ɑ in printing.

Before class begins

1. Tear out the Printing Chart at the back of the student book and display it in a prominent place.

2. Open to page 2.

Lesson

Review the *sound* of the short vowel **a**, showing the flashcard and having the student say the sound several times. Proceed to follow the directions and complete the first exercise on page 2. For the second exercise, consider the first letter in each word and ask if it looks like the ɑ on the flashcard. If so, you and the student should say the short vowel **a** sound and the word; then circle that word. Your excitement and compliments about the student's accomplishments are a great encouragement.

Before the student traces the letters at the bottom of the page, teach the correct way of printing, following the Printing Chart. Have your student practice printing ɑ A on the blackboard or lined paper. For lower case ɑ, first draw the "c" part of the letter, then continue to draw a straight line up and then down on the right side of the letter to complete it.

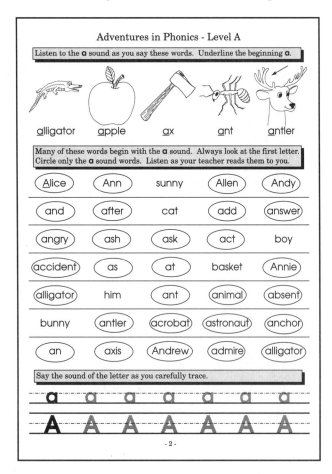

Page 3

Purpose

To become more familiar with the short sound of **a**, discussing that it may be in the middle of a word as well as at the beginning.

Before class begins

Open to page 3.

Lesson

Review the sound of the short vowel **a** with the flashcard. Say the following lists of words, emphasizing the sound of the first letter in each word; see if the student recognizes the word that does not have the short vowel **a** sound in each list.

ant	well	ax	after
apple	animal	bunny	admire
fill	Allen	answer	answer
antler	Alice	ash	mother

Follow the directions and have the student complete the work on the page, "reading" the words several times and putting emphasis on the short sound of "a."

Watch closely that the letters are printed correctly as you have your student practice printing ɑ A on paper or the blackboard.

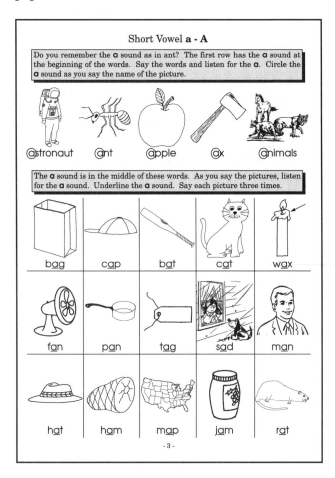

Page 4

Purpose

To better know the sound and formation of the short vowel **a** as it is heard and printed in the middle of words.

Before class begins

Open to page 4.

Lesson

Review the short sound of **a A** with the flashcard five times. Practice printing α ten times on a paper or the blackboard. Point out that the α stands on a "floor" and does not go over the dotted line. After making the "c" part of the α, do not lift the pencil but continue to go up and then straight down.

Discuss and complete page 4, "reading" the words they have completed.

Page 5

Purpose

To begin to teach the recognition and sound of the short vowel **e**.

Before class begins

1. Remove flashcard **e E** from the set of flashcards.
2. Open to page 5, but have it set aside.

Lesson

Review with your student the **a A** flashcard sound, saying it five times. Explain that this letter is called a *vowel* and is a very important letter. Today's lesson teaches another vowel, which has a little different sound. Say the short sound of **e E** several times as your student repeats it after you. We can hear this sound in **e**-lephant, **e**-gg, and **E**-skimo. Drill both flashcards, listening to see if the student can distinguish between the two sounds.

Follow the directions and have the student complete the work on the page.

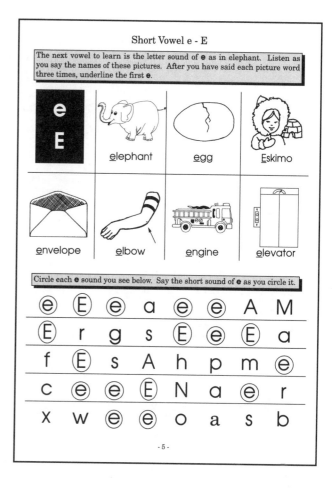

Page 6

Purpose

1. To continue to teach the recognition and sound of the short vowel **e**.

2. To teach proper formation of **e E**.

Before class begins

Open to page 6.

Lesson

Review the sounds of the short vowels **a** and **e** with the flashcards. Say the following lists of words, emphasizing the sound of the first letter in each word; see if the student recognizes the word that does not have the short vowel **e** sound in each list.

edge	enter	empty	elbow
milk	apple	egg	every
ever	Emma	ask	animal
Eddie	Evan	engine	end

Before completing page 6, teach the correct way of printing **e E**, following the Printing Chart. For lower case **e**, first draw a straight line—as on the face of a clock—from the 9 to the 3; without lifting your pencil, continue to draw part of a circle, moving counterclockwise from the 3 to the 4. Encourage and reward neatness.

Page 7

Purpose

To become more familiar with the short sound of **e**, realizing it may be in the middle of a word as well as at the beginning.

Before class begins

Open to page 7.

Lesson

Review the short sounds of **a A** and **e E** with the flashcards, saying them many times. A quick glance back to page 1 as part of the review may be beneficial. With both cards on the table, say words beginning with these vowels to see if the student points to the correct letter (e.g., **a**pple, **e**lephant, **e**gg, **a**x, **a**nt, **E**skimo, **e**nvelope, **a**nchor, **e**lbow, **e**ngine, etc.—as from pages 1 and 5 in the workbook). Be as positive and encouraging as possible.

Follow the directions and complete the lesson, going at a rate you feel best for your child.

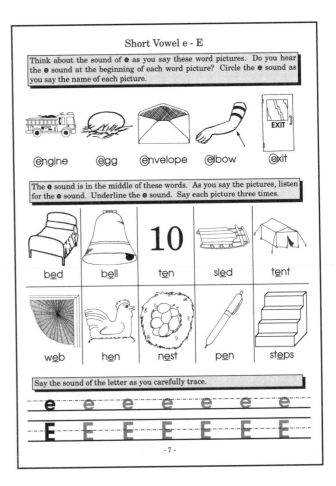

Page 8

Purpose

To review the identity and sound of the short vowel **e** as it is heard and printed in the middle of words.

Before class begins

Open to page 8.

Lesson

While looking at the flashcards, have the child say the sound of the short vowel **e** five times, then the sound of the short vowel **a** five times. Drill the flashcards until he knows them well. Turn back to page 7 and discuss the short vowel **e** in the middle of the words. Can the child hear himself say the **e** sound? Before completing the work on page 8, the student should practice forming the **e** on lined paper or a blackboard.

Follow the directions and have the student complete the work on the page.

Page 9

Purpose

To review the sounds of short **a** and **e** by listening and printing.

Before class begins

Open to page 9.

Lesson

Drill with the flashcards and practice printing the two vowels correctly on paper or blackboard. Before the child prints in the spaces on page 9, have him say each word, listen for the vowel sound, and point to the flashcard that matches the sound. Proceed in this way for each word.

Have your student carefully print the correct vowels ("a" or "e") in the spaces in the middle of the words, as he pronounces them. Also follow the directions at the bottom of the page.

Be ready with appropriate compliments or provide review if necessary.

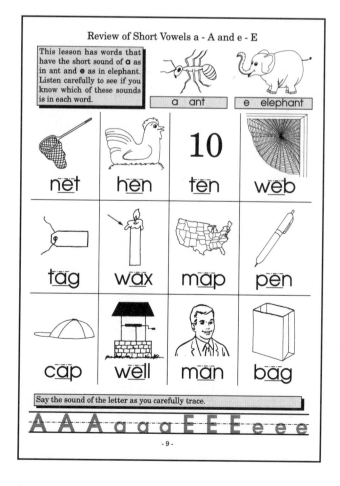

Page 10

Purpose

To review once more the short vowel sounds of **a** and **e**, determining if the student has learned the sounds well.

Before class begins

Open to page 10.

Lesson

If this lesson is done on the same day as page 9 and the child had no difficulty, the flashcard review may not be necessary. If the lesson is done on a following day, review the short vowel sounds of **a** and **e** with flashcards. Have the child go through the lesson first by pointing to the flashcards that match the missing vowels in the middle of the words.

Have your student carefully print the correct vowels ("a" or "e") in the spaces in the middle of the words, as he pronounces them. Also follow the directions at the bottom of the page.

Page 11

Purpose

To teach the recognition and sound of the short vowel **i**.

Before class begins

1. Have short vowel **i I** flashcard ready.

2. Open to page 11.

Lesson

Review the **a** and **e** flashcards. Introduce the short vowel **i** and have the student say it several times. Drill the three vowel flashcards for a short time to make sure that the child can say each of the sounds correctly. Explain that we can hear the short sound of **i** in **i**-nsects, **I**-ndian, and **i**-gloo.

Follow the directions and have the child complete the page.

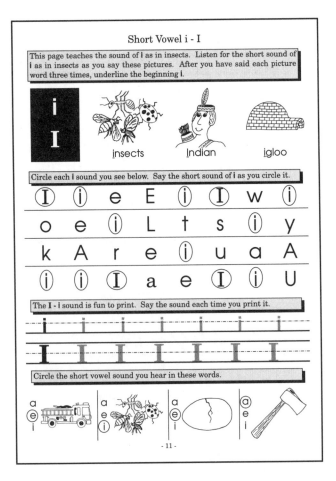

Page 12

Purpose

To continue to teach the recognition and sound of the short vowel **i**.

Before class begins

Open to page 12.

Lesson

Quickly drill the **a**, **e**, and **i** flashcards, having the student say the correct sounds as you flash them then point to the correct letters as you sound them.

Say the following lists of words, emphasizing the sound of the first letter in each word; see if the student recognizes the word that does not have the short vowel **i** sound in each list.

insect	is	invite	inner
apple	inside	elbow	inch
Indian	animal	Italy	igloo
into	itch	image	engine

Consult the Printing Chart as your student practices printing **i I**, encouraging neatness and accuracy.

Have him name the pictures at the top of the page, as he underlines the beginning "i." Follow the directions and complete the rest of the lesson.

Page 13

Purpose

1. To review and confirm the recognition and sound of the short vowel **i**.
2. To be able to distinguish and say the short vowel sounds of **a**, **e**, and **i**.
3. To understand that when the short vowel **i** is written between two consonants, it helps to form a word. (This is true for all the vowels.)

Before class begins

1. Print a row of lower case vowels **a**, **e**, and **i** on a paper or board similar to the following:

   a e i i a e e a i a e e i i

2. Open to page 13.

Lesson

Drill the student by pointing to each vowel that you have printed in the row, having him say the correct sound of each vowel. Continue by asking him to point to the letters and say their sounds, proceeding from left to right. Practice printing the three vowels correctly on the board or lined paper.

Follow the directions and complete page 13.

Page 14

Purpose

To review printing the short vowel sound **i** by placing it in the middle of two consonants to form a word.

Before class begins

Open to page 14.

Lesson

Drill the **a**, **e**, and **i** flashcards if this page is not done on the same day as page 13. Have the student print the vowels on a paper or the board as you dictate each sound (**a, e, a, i, i, a, e, e, i, a, a, e, I, I, A, E, I, I, E, E, A, A, E,** etc.).

Carefully complete this lesson.

Page 15

Purpose

To confirm the short vowel sounds of **a**, **e**, and **i** by knowing the sound that belongs in each word.

Before class begins

Open to page 15.

Lesson

After quickly drilling with flashcards, place the cards on the table and have the student point to the vowel that he hears in each word on page 15. Check the student's printing before he does the work on this page by having him print the vowels on a paper or the board.

Have your student carefully print the correct vowels ("a," "e," or "i") in the spaces in the middle of the words, as he pronounces them. Also follow the directions at the bottom of the page.

Page 16

Purpose

To review the vowels **a**, **e**, and **i** by printing the vowels to form words.

Before class begins

Open to page 16.

Lesson

As in the previous lesson for page 15, proceed in a similar way by placing the flashcards on the table and having the student point to the vowel that he hears in each word on page 16.

Have your student carefully print the correct vowels ("a," "e," or "i") in the spaces in the middle of the words, as he pronounces them. Also follow the directions at the bottom of the page.

After completing this lesson, have the student print the vowels on paper or the board. Encourage neatness by circling the very best letters.

Use this diagram for printing "o." ▶

Page 17

Purpose

To begin to teach the recognition and sound of the short vowel **o**.

Before class begins

1. Have flashcard **o O** ready.
2. Open to page 17.

Lesson

Show your student the **o O** flashcard as you say its short vowel sound. It is heard at the beginning of o-x, o-tter, O-ctober, o-melet, o-dd, O-ntario, and o-n. Have him notice your mouth as you say the sound of the short vowel **o**.

By way of review, drill with the four vowel flashcards until you determine that the student knows them well. Have him pronounce the correct sounds as you flash the cards, then have him point to the correct letters as you sound them.

Next teach the correct way of printing **o O**, following the Printing Chart. It is best to begin forming the **o O** by thinking about the 2 on the face of a clock and proceeding backward to the 2 again.

Follow the directions and complete page 13.

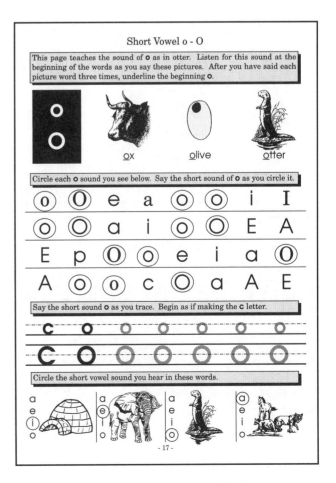

Page 18

Purpose

To continue to teach the recognition and sound of the short vowel **o**, being able to see and hear it at the beginning of words.

Before class begins

Open to page 18.

Lesson

Drill with the flashcards for the vowels **a**, **e**, **i**, and **o**. Pronounce words beginning with each of the vowels and ask the student to print the correct vowel on the board. You may want to use the following words:

a-stronaut	**o**-x	**i**-nch	**A**-ndrew
a-nimal	**e**-dge	**i**-nform	**o**-pposite
E-sther	**i**-ll	**O**-scar	**I**-ndiana

You may also use the words in the second exercise on page 18. Remind your student that proper names begin with upper case, or capital letters.

Follow the directions and complete page 18.

Page 19

Purpose

To become more familiar with the short sound of **o**, teaching that it may often be found in the middle of short words as well as at the beginning of short and long words.

Before class begins

Open to page 19.

Lesson

Quickly drill the four flashcards, remembering to give a cheerful compliment for correct answers and a gentle correction for any wrong ones. Place the flashcards on the table. Say words with emphasis on the vowels, and ask the student to point to the correct vowel. You may want to use the following words:

c**a**t	**e**gg	**i**tch	c**a**p	b**o**x	s**i**t	fl**o**p
h**i**ll	c**o**b	p**a**t	p**e**t	p**i**t	p**o**t	t**a**sk
n**e**st	f**e**ll	w**e**ll	w**i**ll	h**a**t	h**o**t	h**i**t

Follow the directions and complete page 19.

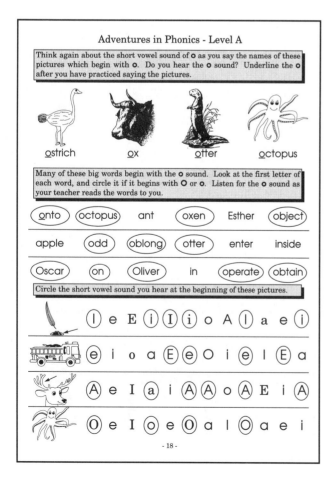

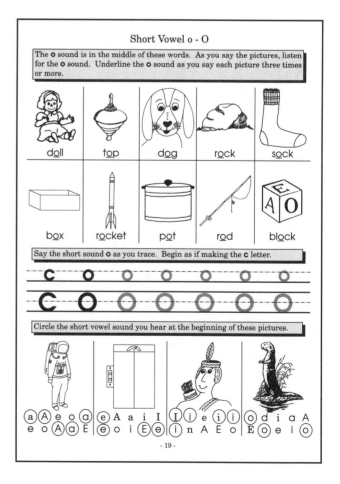

Page 20

Purpose

To review the identity and sound of the short vowel **o** as it is found in the middle of words.

Before class begins

Open to page 20.

Lesson

By way of review, drill your student with the **a**, **e**, **i**, and **o** flashcards. Have him pronounce the correct sounds as you flash the cards, then have him point to the correct letters as you sound them. Also have him practice printing these four vowels (**a A, e E, i I,** and **o O**) on lined paper or the board.

Follow the directions and complete page 20.

Page 21

Purpose

To review the four short vowel sounds of **a**, **e**, **i**, and **o**, checking to see if the student knows the sound and proper formation of each one.

Before class begins

Open to page 21.

Lesson

Quickly drill with the **a**, **e**, **i**, and **o** flashcards. Have the student pronounce the correct sounds as you flash the cards, then have him point to the correct letters as you sound them.

Before the student completes this lesson, have him point to the correct flashcard as he hears each short vowel word sounded on page 21.

Have your student carefully print the correct vowels ("a," "e," "i," or "o") in the spaces in the middle of the words, as he pronounces them. Also follow the directions at the bottom of the page.

Have your student "read" the words several times after he has completed the page, asking him to emphasize the vowels with his voice. Since every word must have a vowel, explain to your student that he has just made these sets of letters into words by printing the correct vowels in the blanks.

Page 22

Purpose

To review once more the short vowel sounds of **a**, **e**, **i**, and **o**.

Before class begins

Open to page 22.

Lesson

If this lesson is completed on a separate day from page 21, quickly drill with the vowel flashcards of **a**, **e**, **i**, and **o**. As mentioned in previous instructions, work the page twice by having the student correctly point to the letters at the top of the page or to the flashcards, determining whether he knows the correct sound of the short vowels found in the middle of these words.

Have your student carefully print the correct vowels ("a," "e," "i," or "o") in the spaces in the middle of the words, as he pronounces them.

Page 23

Purpose

To teach the recognition and sound of the short vowel **u**.

Before class begins

1. Have the short vowel **u U** flashcard ready.
2. Open to page 23.

Lesson

Discuss the sound and shape of the short vowel **u**, using the **u U** flashcard. Explain that we can hear this sound in **u**-mbrella, **u**-p, and **u**-mpire. Quickly drill with the five vowel flashcards in a fun, but attentive manner.

Test to see if the student has learned these letters by having him point to the correct flashcard as you say words like the following:

i-nch	**e**-gg	**u**-nder	**A**-frica	**o**-lives
i-nto	**u**-ntil	**u**-nfair	**E**-dward	**A**-dam
O-scar	**i**-gloo	**u**-ncle	**a**-nimal	**i**-nfect

Next teach the correct way of printing **u U**, following the Printing Chart. Have your student practice its formation on lined paper or the board.

Follow directions and complete page 23.

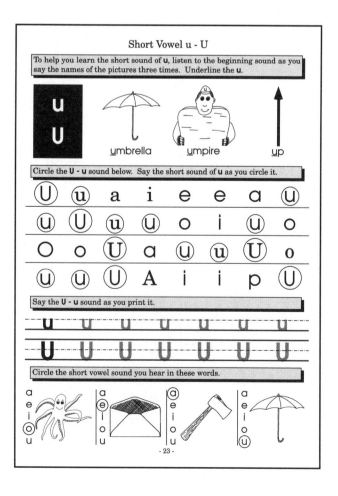

Page 24

Purpose

To review the identity and sound of the short vowel **u** as it is found at the beginning of words.

Before class begins

Open to page 24.

Lesson

Drill with the flashcards for the vowels **a**, **e**, **i**, **o**, and **u**. For variety, have your student draw an **umbrella**, **egg**, **apple**, **Indian**, and **olive** on a paper or the board; then have him point to the correct flashcard that matches the beginning, short vowel sound as you name the picture.

Follow directions and complete page 24.

Page 25

Purpose

To become more familiar with the short vowel sound of **u**, as it appears in the middle of words and at the beginning of short or long words.

Before class begins

Open to page 25.

Lesson

Quickly drill with the vowel flashcards of **a**, **e**, **i**, **o**, and **u**. Review the use of these vowels in the middle of short vowel words by having the student point to the correct flashcard as you say words such as the following:

sit	pan	rob	hum	bell	hit
hut	hat	hot	hem	tub	nut

Before your student completes this lesson, have him draw a picture of a **sun**, **tub**, and **bug** on a paper or the board. Discuss the middle sound of **u** as you print the word under each of his pictures.

Follow the directions and complete page 25.

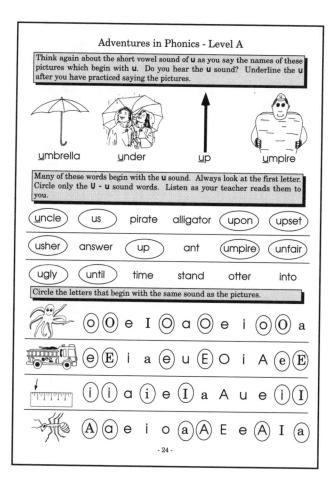

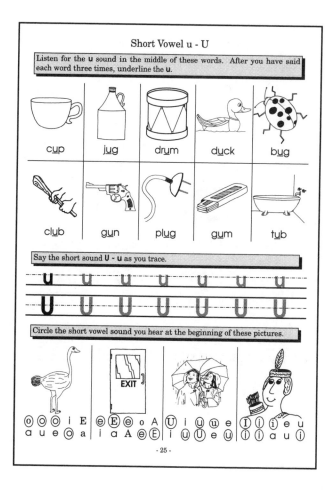

Page 26

Purpose

To review the identity and sound of the short vowel **u** as it is found in the middle of words.

Before class begins

Open to page 26.

Lesson

Drill by having the child point to the flashcards on display as you say the sounds. Have him print each sound, lower case and capital, on the board or paper, checking to see proper formation.

Go over page 26 orally and say the words before the student carefully prints in the "u."

Page 27

Purpose

To review each of the short vowel sounds by properly printing the correct vowel in the middle of words.

Before class begins

Open to page 27.

Lesson

Quickly drill with the **a**, **e**, **i**, **o**, and **u** flashcards. Have the student pronounce the correct sounds as you flash the cards, then have him point to the correct letters as you sound them.

Place all of the cards next to each other before the student. Have him go over each word in the lesson by pointing to the card that tells the sound of the missing letter.

Have your student carefully print the correct vowels ("a," "e," "i," "o," or "u") in the spaces in the middle of the words, as he pronounces them. Watch for the correct formation of the letters.

Note that the second image in the last row on page 27 could be answered "Jan" or "Jen"; either answer is acceptable.

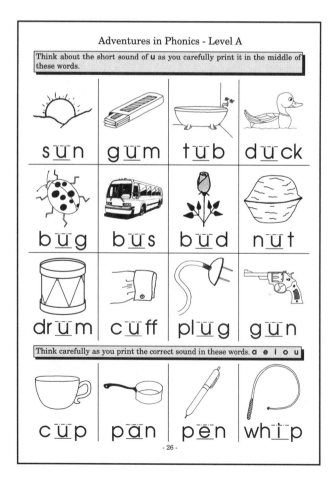

Page 28

Purpose

To provide additional review of all the vowel sounds by printing them in the middle of words.

Before class begins

Open to page 28.

Lesson

If this page is done on the same day as the previous page, just continue to follow the same directions in completing the written work. If it is completed on a separate day, begin with a quick flashcard drill.

Have your student carefully print the correct vowels ("a," "e," "i," "o," or "u") in the spaces in the middle of the words, as he pronounces them. Watch for the correct formation of the letters.

Note that the image in the lower left-hand corner of the page may represent "pet" or "pat"; either answer is acceptable.

Page 29

Purpose

To begin teaching the sound and formation of the consonant s.

Before class begins

Open to page 29 and have flashcard s S ready to add to the short vowel flashcards.

Lesson

Briefly discuss that the letters belong in two different groups: *consonants* and *vowels*.

The short sounds of the vowels have been learned, and today the first of the consonants will be learned. The s is fun to say and print. The capital is just bigger than the lower case. The words Saviour, salvation, Scripture, Spirit, sin, and sermon begin with s. Read the following sentences:

See Susan sew some suits for seven sisters.

Sammy sat still as six seagulls swooped and stopped to snatch some snacks.

Follow directions and complete page 29.

After completing the lesson, quickly drill all of the flashcards. Then have your student practice additional printing of s S on the board or lined paper.

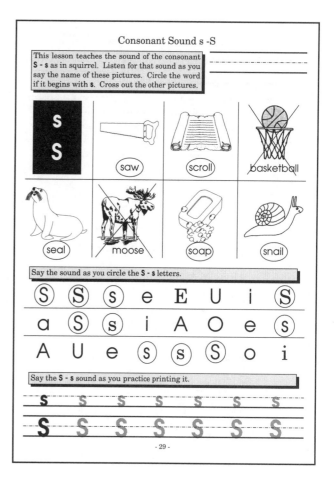

Page 30

Purpose

1. To become more familiar with the sound and identity of **s** as it appears at the beginning of words.

2. To begin a new and important practice of saying the **s** with the vowels, which is a first big step in learning to read!

Before class begins

Open to page 30.

Lesson

Warm up with a quick drill of the flashcards. Have the student practice forming **s S** on lined paper or the board.

Complete page 30 carefully, encouraging the student whenever possible.

If more practice is needed, review the center section of the lesson by reading **sa**, **se**, **si**, **so**, and **su**.

Page 31

Purpose

To begin teaching the sound and formation of the consonant **t**.

Before class begins

Open to page 31 and have flashcard **t T** ready.

Lesson

Ask the student "What can we use to talk to someone far away?" "What may we look at to see special programs or the news?" "What do we want to know if we look at a clock?" "What big bird says 'gobble, gobble'?" Print **t T** on the board or lined paper, or show the **t T** flashcard and discuss the sound this consonant makes. Ask if he can hear the beginning sound of these words:

tongue	teach	tiger	toes	turkey
Tuesday	tulip	tummy		Testament
Tommy	tooth	table		tabernacle

Add the **t T** flashcard to the others and drill.

Look at the blue box at the top of the page. The top letter **t** is how people print it; the middle letter **T**, or capital letter, is used for proper names as in Timothy or Tyler; and the bottom letter **t** is how many computers and word processors print it.

Complete page 31.

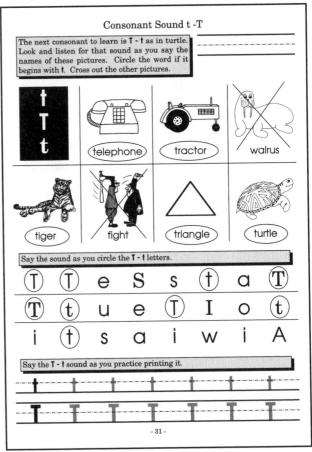

Page 32

Purpose

1. To become more familiar with the sound and identity of **t** as it comes at the beginning of words.

2. To teach the student to say the **t** with each vowel.

Lesson

After a quick drill with the flashcards, ask the student to print the consonants **s** and **t** on the board or lined paper.

Lay all the flashcards on the table. Ask the student to point to the sound heard at the beginning of these words:

Samson   Timothy   Adam   Esther   Sarah

temple   umbrella   into   enter   Oscar

Follow the directions and complete page 32.

When done, see if your student can print the following sets of letters and words on lined paper:

ti	su	te	so	ta	tu	to
sa-t		si-t		se-t		te-st

Be very encouraging. If this exercise is too difficult, patiently demonstrate how to print the words. Save this paper as a record of his initial printing work.

Page 33

Purpose

To begin to teach the sound and formation of the consonant **b**.

Before class begins

Open to page 33 and have flashcard **b B** ready.

Lesson

Ask your student, "What is the most important book God wants us to read?" (Bible) "Yes, now look at this **b B** flashcard, and listen to many other wonderful things God wants us to enjoy: bananas, berries, beautiful butterflies, beans, bread, butter, bees, birds, beetles, bugs, beets, beagles, bears, and babies." Listen as he repeats the **b** sound after you say it. Show how it is made by drawing it on the board or lined paper following the Printing Chart.

First talk about the whole page with the student, doing the work orally. Then follow the directions to complete the lesson.

If more practice is needed, do a quick drill with the flashcards of all the letters that have been introduced. Also practice printing **b B** on lined paper.

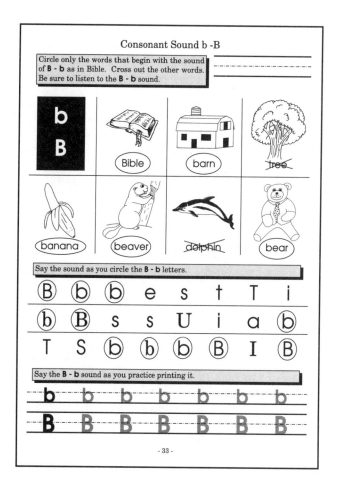

Page 34

Purpose

1. To become better acquainted with the sound and formation of **b**, and to be able to say **b** with short vowels and read *whole* words for the first time.

2. To recognize consonant sounds of words beginning with **s**, **t**, and **b**.

Lesson

Quickly drill the flashcards. Print **ba**, **be**, **bi**, **bo**, and **bu** on the board or paper and have the student practice saying them. If needed, say the sound and have your student repeat it after you as you begin this exercise. Then have the student point to the letter of the sound you say to him.

Work your way through page 34 by first having the student point to the answers. Then have the student do the work with a pencil. For the exercise at the bottom of the page, have the student say the names of the pictures and circle the letter that comes at the *beginning* of each word.

Additional printing helps reinforce what your student is learning. On lined paper, print the letter **b** for him to practice. Also help him print the following words:

bat   tab   but   bit   tub

Keep it in a folder for his records.

Page 35

Purpose

To introduce the sound and formation of the consonant **h**.

Before class begins

Open to page 35 and have flashcard **h H** ready.

Lesson

Ask your child, "Where will we live forever with Jesus if we love Him?" (Heaven) "Each time we say this letter we let breath out of our mouth." Show the **h** flashcard, and ask the student to repeat the following sentences after you:

Hannah was so happy to have her baby Samuel.

Helen saw Henry, Herbert, and Harvey help Harold haul the heavy horse.

A huge helicopter hovered over the house on the high hill.

Do the work on page 35 orally before completing it in pencil. The student should be able to easily learn how to print this letter.

Remember to compliment whenever it is appropriate. Everyone will be happy.

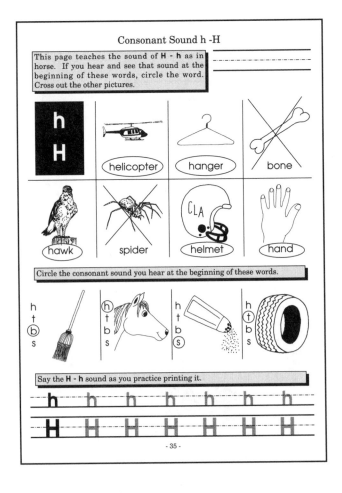

Page 36

Purpose

To become better acquainted with the sound and formation of **h**, and to get practice in sounding the consonant with the short vowels.

Lesson

Have a quick flashcard drill of all the letters that the student has learned. After you print the following words on the board or a paper, help the student try to sound them out. Perhaps you could have the student practice printing these words on lined paper:

hat	has	hit
his	hot	hut

Complete page 36, working the bottom section orally before using a pencil.

Work slowly and patiently, encouraging him as much as possible.

Note that the third image in the last row on page 36 may be thought of as a "hotdog" or "bun," so the student may circle either the **h** or **b**, respectively.

Page 37

Purpose

To begin to teach the sound and formation of the consonant **f**.

Before class begins

Open to page 37 and have flashcard **f F** ready.

Lesson

Say to your child, "A funny sound comes out between our top teeth and bottom lip as this new sound is made. Fred and his father proudly flew their flag from the front porch for the Fourth of July. Francis found five fine feathers that had fallen as a flock of birds flew over the fence. To have friends, one must be friendly."

Have the student repeat the sound several times as you show how to print it, using the Printing Chart. Add the **f F** flashcard to the others and quickly drill.

Say the following words which have the **f** sound in the middle or at the end of them: muffin, coffee, puffing, leaf, cuff, loaf, calf, roof.

Follow directions and complete page 37.

Have the student get additional practice by printing **f** on lined paper. He should begin drawing—as on the face of a clock—at the 2, moving back toward the 12 and then straight down to the 6; then draw a short crossbar (line) through the vertical part of the letter.

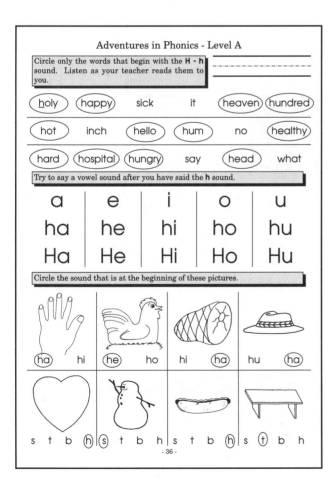

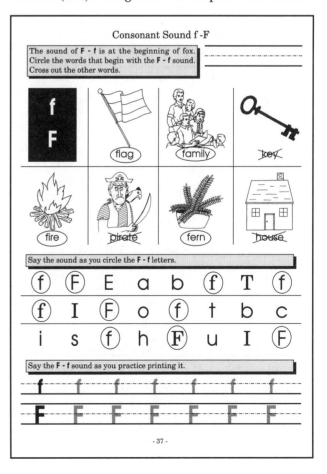

Page 38

Purpose

To become more familiar with the sound and identity of **f**, and to practice saying the **f** before the short vowel sounds.

Lesson

Begin with a quick flashcard exercise, perhaps with the student pointing to the correct cards spread in front of him as you say the sounds. Help the child to practice printing **f F** and to print the following words on the board or lined paper labeled "**f**":

fat   fit   fast

If this is too difficult, patiently demonstrate how to print these words.

Do the work on page 38 with the student orally. Then have him go over it a second time and write the answers with a pencil.

A child still needs direct supervision and immediate responses ("yes" or "no") to his answers. Be generous with encouragement, compliment him for correct answers, and be gentle with corrections.

Page 39

Purpose

To introduce the sound and formation of the consonant **m**.

Before class begins

Open to page 39 and have flashcard **m M** ready.

Lesson

Holding the **m M** flashcard, show with your lips how this letter is pronounced in the following sentences:

Mary's **m**other **m**ade **m**eatballs on **M**onday.

Molly **m**ade a **m**ess and **m**ust **m**op.

Many **m**en played **m**arvelous **m**usic at the **m**arriage of **M**ichael and **M**artha.

Quickly drill all the flashcards.

Complete page 39.

Have the student get additional practice by printing **m M** on lined paper. Help the student print the following words as you slowly say them:

mat   met   am   mom   ham
him   hem   hum   Sam   Tim

If possible, leave these words on the board or hang up the paper to review before doing page 40.

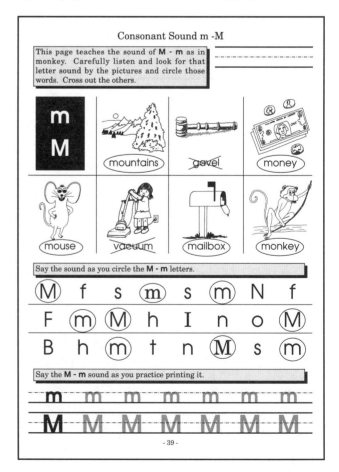

Page 40

Purpose

1. To continue learning the sound and identity of the consonant **m**.

2. To review the sounds of consonants **s**, **t**, **b**, **h**, and **f**.

Lesson

Begin by having the student print the capital and lower case forms of **m M** on lined paper. Then practice reading the words from the exercise for page 39, which were written on the board or a paper. Pronounce the following words to teach that **m** may also be in the middle of words:

summer   coming   hammer   lamp

hump   numbers   woman   stamp

Complete the work on page 40 with the student orally before doing the work in pencil. For the second exercise, have the student say the names of the pictures and circle the letter that comes at the *beginning* of each word.

Page 41

Purpose

To introduce the formation and **k** sound of consonants c and k.

Before class begins

Open to page 41 and have flashcards c C and k K ready.

Lesson

With both flashcards in view, say the sound that both consonants can make and read this sentence:

Kathy and Carl called Kevin and Carol to come to see their cat's cute kittens.

Many words that are delicious foods to eat begin with the **k** sound. Read the following sentences:

Keith planted carrots, cabbage, cauliflower, corn, and currants in his garden.

Be careful not to eat too many candies, cupcakes, cookies, or caramels.

The kind king carefully cared for his kingdom.

For the exercise at the top of the page, have the student say the names of the pictures and circle the words that begin with the sound of "k" and cross out the word that does not. Carefully complete the rest of page 41.

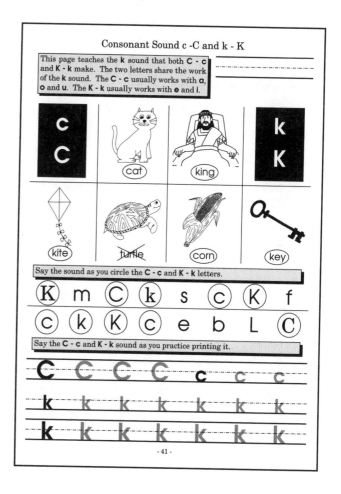

Page 42

Purpose

To become better acquainted with the sounds and formations of **c** and **k**, and to review consonants **s**, **t**, **b**, **h**, **f**, and **m**.

Lesson

Quickly drill the vowel flashcards and then the consonant flashcards. Have the student practice printing the **c C** and **k K** on the board or lined paper. Ask the question: "What can we not eat from the following group of words?"

ketchup	**K**ansas	**c**oolwhip	**c**urtains
cantaloupe	**c**orn	**k**itchen	**c**aramels
California	**c**andy	**c**ookies	**c**arrot

Read these sentences aloud to your student:

Conrad's **c**ollie **c**an **c**onsume a **c**omplete **c**an of dog food.

God **c**reated all of the wonderful **c**reatures such as the **c**rocodile, **c**ricket, **c**row, **c**ougar, **c**ondor, **c**ockatoo, **k**angaroo, **k**iwi, **k**udu, **k**oala, **c**amel, **c**ow, **k**atydid, and **c**aterpillar.

After practicing the exercise at the top of page 42, have your student do the next exercise orally and then complete the lesson with pencil.

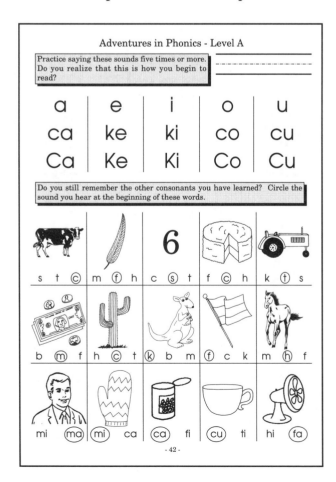

Page 43

Purpose

To introduce the formation and sound of the consonant **d**.

Before class begins

Open to page 43 and have flashcard **d D** ready.

Lesson

Quickly drill the consonant flashcards, especially reviewing the **b B** flashcard. Showing flashcard **d D**, say the sound it makes and read these sentences:

Daniel **d**id not **d**isobey and was **d**elivered by God from being **d**estroyed by the lions in the **d**en.

David's **d**og **d**igs **d**eep holes in the **d**irt.

Ask these questions:

1. What coin is the same as 10 cents? (*dime*)
2. Who checks and cleans our teeth? (*dentist*)
3. What toy is a favorite of little girls? (*doll*)
4. What bird makes quacking sounds? (*duck*)
5. How does good food taste? (*delicious*)
6. What barks and wags his tail? (*dog*)

Practice printing **d D** on the board or lined paper.

Have your student complete page 43 and read the sentence under the picture of Sam and his desk.

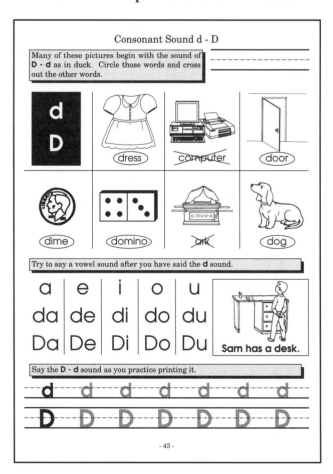

Page 44

Purpose

To become more familiar with the formation and sound of **d** and to review consonants **s, t, b, h, f, m, c,** and **k.**

Lesson

Drill all the consonants above by standing the flashcards against a support and asking the student to point to the consonant that he hears at the beginning of the following words:

bat	map	hand	sun	fish	doll	cat
kit	sun	horse	fast	ball	cow	top
kite	toe	hat	sit	fun	door	man

If there is confusion between **b** and **d**, show that the capital **B** and lower case **b** have circles facing the same way. Putting up a paper with **b** next to a picture of a **ball** and **d** next to a picture of a **dog** may help. Daily review and gentle correction will help in learning the difference. Help the student to print the following words on lined paper labeled "**d**":

dot	dim	did	sad	bad
cod	dad	had	dab	bud

First complete page 44 orally, then with a pencil.

Page 45

Purpose

To teach the formation and sound of the consonant **j.**

Before class begins

Open to page 45 and have flashcard **j J** ready.

Lesson

Show the flashcard and say "Our new sound is heard at the beginning of the name Jesus." Teach how to print **j J** on the board or lined paper.

Have the student repeat after you some of the other names that come from the Bible: Jehovah, Joseph, Jonah, James, Jacob, Jesse, Joshua, Judah, Jeremiah, Job, John, Jehoshaphat, Jael, Jezebel, and Joel.

Also read these sentences aloud to your student:

Julie was joyful to join our class.

January, June, and July are months.

Jemimah eats too much jello, jam, and jelly.

Joey saw the jack rabbit jump into a hole.

Jane is not jealous of Judy.

Something jingled in the pocket of John's jacket.

Complete the work on page 45.

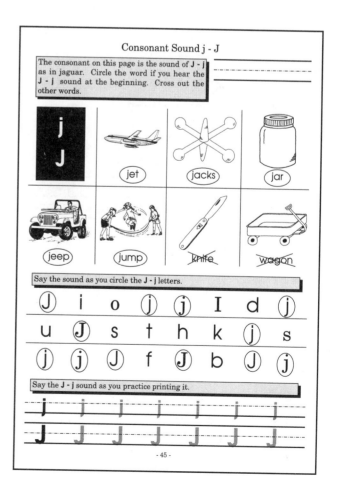

Page 46

Purpose

To become better acquainted with the formation and sound of **j** and review the previously learned consonants.

Lesson

After reviewing the correct way to print **j J** on the board or lined paper labeled "**j**," help the student to print the following words:

jet	jam	jab	job
Jim	Jan	Jed	just

Leave the words on the board or paper to review after completing page 46. Remember to give compliments whenever possible. Lean the flashcards on a support and drill the cards by having the student point to the correct card as you say the sound of each consonant and vowel.

Carefully go over page 46 orally with your student. For the first exercise, have him print the correct letter of the sound at the beginning of each word represented by the row of pictures. Then have him complete the rest of the lesson.

Page 47

Purpose

To begin to teach the formation and sound of consonant **r**.

Before class begins

Open to page 47 and have flashcard **r R** ready.

Lesson

While showing the flashcard **r R**, listen carefully as the student repeats the following sentences, after you say them:

Ruth was a **r**eaper.

Ralph's **r**ed **r**oses are **r**eally beautiful.

Robert's **r**ubber **r**aft **r**ocked and made a **r**ipple on the **r**iver.

Richard saw a **r**ainbow above his **r**oof.

Rena's **r**uby **r**ing **r**olled under a **r**ound **r**ock.

Teach how the letter **r R** should be formed, using the Printing Chart.

Quickly drill the flashcards, putting the ones that are said correctly facedown.

Complete page 47.

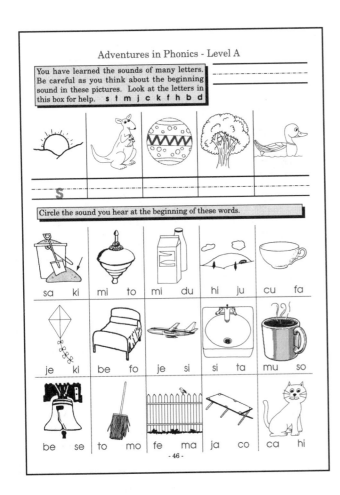

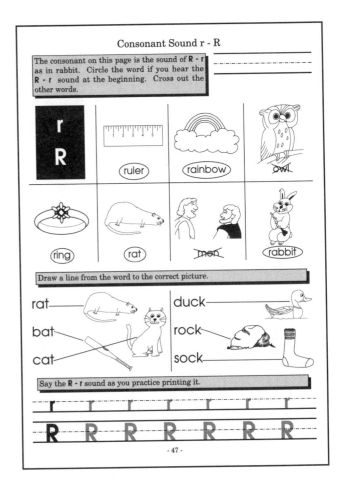

Page 48

Purpose

To confirm the sound and formation of the consonant **r** as well as review all flashcards from previous lessons.

Lesson

After a brief practice in printing **r R** on the blackboard or lined paper labeled "**r**," help the student to print the following words:

rat	rob	rib	rest
red	rub	rim	rust

Have the student listen as you pronounce words ending with the **r** sound:

star   far   car   bar   winter   or
door   purr   fur   sir   summer   jar

Review all flashcards quickly.

Complete page 48 by first answering orally before doing the work with pencil. For the exercise at the bottom half of the page, have the student say the names of the pictures and circle the letter that comes at the *end* of each word.

Note that the image at the end of the first row in the second exercise represents *golf*, not a golf *club*.

Page 49

Purpose

To introduce the sound and formation of the consonant **g**.

Before class begins

Open to page 49 and have **g G** flashcard ready.

Lesson

As you hold the **g G** flashcard and tell the sound it makes, say "Our **g**reat and **g**racious **G**od made every **g**ood thing."

Ask the student to repeat the following sentences after you say them to check for correct pronunciation:

Grace **g**ave **g**old **g**ifts to the **g**ood **g**irls.

Gray **g**eese **g**ot **g**oodies from the **g**arden.

Grant's **g**oat **g**obbled **g**reen **g**rapes and **g**rass.

Teach how to print **g G**, and have the student practice on the board or lined paper labeled "**g**." Help him to print these words:

God   gas   get   gift   got   gum

Complete page 49. For the exercise at the top of the page, have the student say the names of the pictures and circle the words that begin with the sound of "g," besides coloring their pictures. Also cross out the word(s) that do not begin with "g."

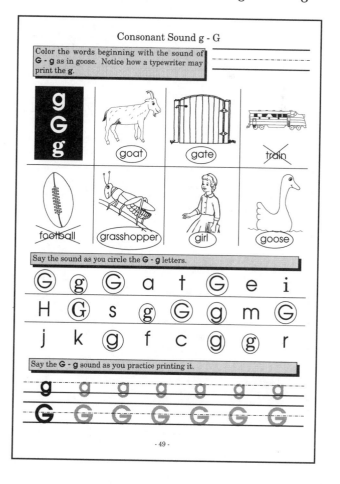

Page 50

Purpose

To continue to teach the sound and formation of **g** and review the consonants previously learned.

Lesson

After a time of quickly drilling the flashcards and printing **g G** on the board or lined paper, help the student print the following words:

rag	tag	mug	tug	bug	big
bag	beg	dig	hug	rug	fig

Complete the work on page 50.

Page 51

Purpose

To teach the sound and formation of the consonant l.

Before class begins

Open to page 51 and have flashcard l L ready.

Lesson

Here are some examples to say to your child:

The Lord is my light. I love the law of the Lord.

The Bible is a lamp and a light for my life.

Larry laughed loudly as his lambs leaped lightly over leaves on the lawn.

Lights lit the lobby as Lars lugged luggage and linens.

An important lesson to teach is that the l is doubled when it comes at the end of short vowel words. Write the following words on the board or lined paper:

bell	dell	fell	hell	sell	tell
bill	fill	gill	hill	kill	mill
doll	dull	gull	hull	lull	mull

Have your student repeat these words after you and print them on lined paper or the board.

Complete the work on page 51.

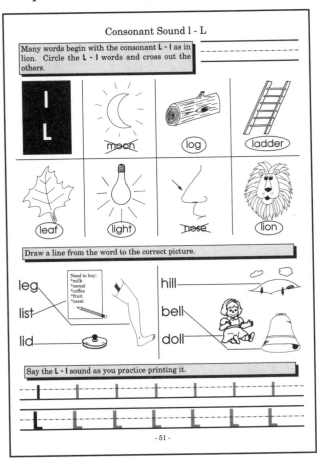

Page 52

Purpose

To become more familiar with the sound and formation of the consonant **l**, as well as review the consonants from previous lessons.

Lesson

Quickly drill all the flashcards learned through consonant **l**.

Do the work on the top half of page 52. On the lower half, have the student read both words in the box and point to the answer before he completes the work independently with a pencil.

Help the student to print the following words on the board or lined paper labeled "l":

leg   last   lot   list   let   lock   lad

See how well he will do in spelling the following words ending with double l.

bell	dell	fell	hell	sell	tell
bill	fill	gill	hill	kill	mill
Bill	Jill	drill	rill	sill	till
doll	dull	gull	hull	lull	mull

Page 53

Purpose

To begin teaching the sound and formation of the consonant **n**.

Before class begins

Open to page 53 and have **n N** flashcard ready.

Lesson

As you hold the **n N** flashcard, tell your student the sound this letter makes and teach him how to correctly print it. Ask him, "What rhyming words, beginning with **n**, answer the following riddles?"

Sit on my lap, and take a (**nap**).	Ned bought a pickle for just one (**nickel**).
The white purse belonged to a (**nurse**).	Nancy smelled a rose with her (**nose**).

Help the student print the following words on a blackboard or lined paper labeled "n":

nab	nag	nap	neck	nest	net
nick	nill	nip	nod	not	nut

For the exercise at the top of page 53, have the student say the names of the pictures and circle the words that begin with the sound of "n," as well as coloring their pictures, and cross out the words that do not. Have him read the sentence under the picture of Sam and complete the page.

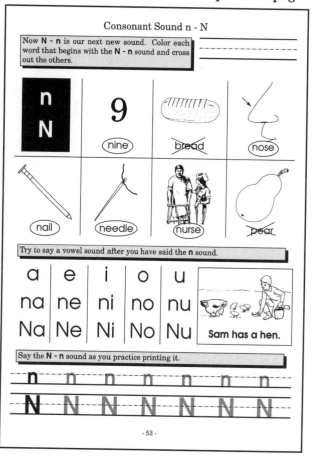

Page 54

Purpose

To consider once more the sound and formation of **n**, to build many new words, and to review the consonants from previous lessons.

Lesson

Quickly drill all flashcards from past lessons. Help the student to print the following words on the blackboard or lined paper:

man	can	run	den	sin	sun
fun	ten	tent	fan	not	men
Ned	Jan	Nan	Dan	Don	Jill

Complete page 54 by first answering orally before doing the work with pencil. For the exercise at the bottom half of the page, have the student say the names of the pictures and circle the letter that come at the *end* of each word.

Page 55

Purpose

To begin to teach the formation and sound of the consonant **w**.

Before class begins

Open to page 55 and have flashcard **w W** ready.

Lesson

Show the **w W** flashcard and say, "This letter is fun to draw. The capital and lower case look alike. We draw down, up, down, up."

Tell your student to watch, listen, and say after you the following sentences:

God made our wonderful world with many places beginning with W: Washington, West Point, Westminster, Wyoming, Winnipeg, Williamsburg, Wittenburg, and Wisconsin.

Wendy and William watched a woman wash wide windows with water from the well on Wednesday in West Wellington.

Have your student practice printing **w W** on lined paper, using the Printing Chart as a guide.

Complete page 55.

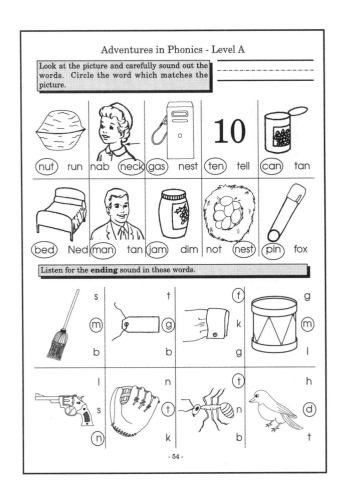

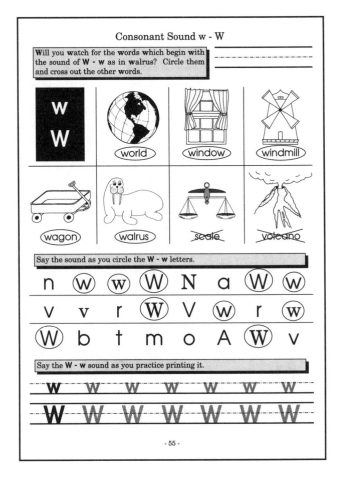

Page 56

Purpose

To review the sound and formation of **w**, as well as review consonants from previous lessons.

Lesson

Quickly drill the consonant flashcards, giving special attention to **w**. On lined paper labeled "**w**" help the student to practice printing this letter, as well as the following words:

win	will	well	wag	west
web	wed	wig	wet	went

Have the student give the answers orally before using a pencil to complete page 56.

Page 57

Purpose

To begin to teach the formation and sound of the consonant **p**.

Before class begins

Open to page 57 and have flashcard **p P** ready.

Lesson

Hold up the **p P** flashcard and say that our lips come together as we begin to make the sound of this consonant.

Read these sentences aloud:

We **p**raise God in our **p**rayers for his **p**erfect **p**lans.

Peter and **P**aul **p**acked **p**lenty of food for a **p**icnic in the **p**ark in **P**ennsylvania. They brought **p**op, **p**ickles, **p**otato chips, **p**eanuts, **P**opsicles, **p**ears, **p**izza, **p**retzels, **p**eaches, **p**umpkin **p**ie, and **p**opcorn.

Teach the student to print **p P** and help him spell the following words on the blackboard or lined paper labeled "**p**":

pan	pen	pin	pad	pill	pop
pit	Pat	pot	pod	pig	pup

Complete page 57.

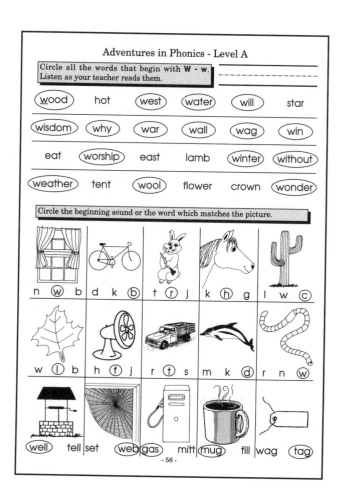

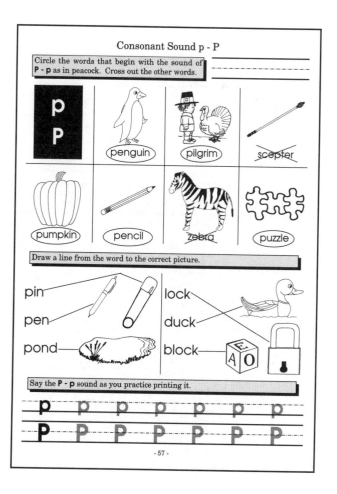

Page 58

Purpose

To continue to teach the formation and sound of the consonant **p** and to review the sounds of consonants from previous lessons.

Lesson

Quickly drill the consonant and vowel flashcards separately. Have your student practice printing the **p P** on the lined paper. Help him to read the words he wrote for page 57 and then print these words:

map	mop	hop	top	tap	tip
rip	sip	hip	lip	dip	nip

On page 58, help your student to say the answers orally and then do the work with a pencil. For the second exercise, have the student say the names of the pictures and circle the letter that comes at the *beginning* of each word.

Remember to give compliments and encouragement each day. Does your student see enthusiasm in your attitude?

Page 59

Purpose

To teach the sound and formation of the consonant **v**.

Before class begins

Open to page 59 and have flashcard **v V** ready.

Lesson

As you show the **v V** flashcard and say its sound, have the student listen as you say these sentences:

Victoria and Virginia visited Valerie's vineyard and vegetable garden in a vacant lot in the village down in a valley.

Verna put violets and vines in a very nice vase and vacuumed the floors.

Victor put his violin in his van.

Teach the student how to print **v V**, using the Printing Chart.

Complete page 59.

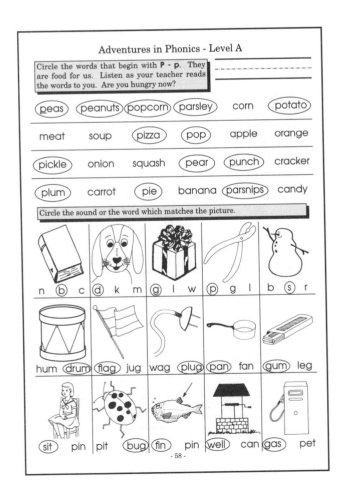

Page 60

Purpose

1. To reinforce the sound and formation of the consonant **v**.
2. To review the other consonant sounds from previous lessons.

Lesson

Quickly drill the vowel and consonant flashcards. Have the student practice printing **v V** on lined paper or the board and spell these words:

van   vest   vet   vast   vent

Go over page 60 orally before doing the work with a pencil. For the exercise at the bottom of the page, have the student say the names of the pictures and circle the letter that comes at the *end* of each word.

Page 61

Purpose

To teach the sound and formation of the consonant **q** which usually has the vowel **u** following it.

Before class begins

Open to page 61 and have flashcard **qu Qu** ready.

Lesson

As you hold up the **qu Qu** flashcard and say its sound (**kw**), ask the student to repeat the following words, after you pronounce them:

question   quite   quiver   quick   quill
quart   quartz   quarter   quail   quest

1. In the Bible, Esther was a (*queen*).
2. A short test may be called a (*quiz*).
3. The sound that a duck makes is (*quack*).
4. If baby is sleeping, we should be (*quiet*).
5. A warm blanket made of many pieces of material sewn together is called a (*quilt*).

Teach the student to print **qu Qu** on the board or paper, using the Printing Chart.

For the exercise at the top of page 61, have the student say the names of the pictures, circle the words that begin with the sound of "qu," and cross out the words that do not. Complete the lesson.

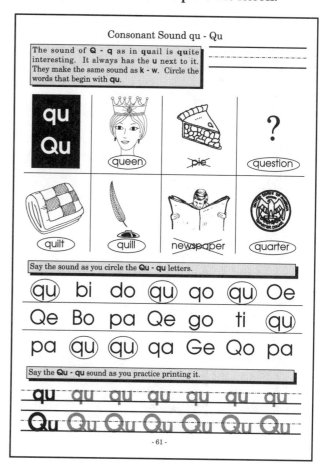

Page 62

Purpose

1. To reinforce the sound and formation of **qu**.
2. To review previously learned consonants.

Lesson

Quickly drill the flashcards, checking that the sounds are pronounced correctly.

After completing the exercise the top of page 62, work the bottom exercise on the page orally before asking the student to complete the answers independently.

Note that the first two rows of the exercise at the bottom of the page require the student to circle the sound of the *first* letter(s) in each word represented by the pictures.

Be ready with gentle corrections and happy compliments.

Help the student to print these **qu** words:

quilt   quit   quill   quick

Page 63

Purpose

To begin to teach the sound and formation of the consonant **y**.

Before class begins

Open to page 63 and have **y Y** flashcard ready.

Lesson

Hold up the **y Y** flashcard and say the sound several times, listening as the student says it. Say that this is the sound **y** makes when it is at the beginning of words such as in the following sentences:

You may play in the **y**ard with the **y**o-**y**o.

The **y**olk of an egg is **y**ellow.

Yesterday a **y**oung man **y**elled to the **y**ak.

You should honor the Lord in **y**our **y**outh.

Complete page 63.

Have the student practice printing **y Y**.

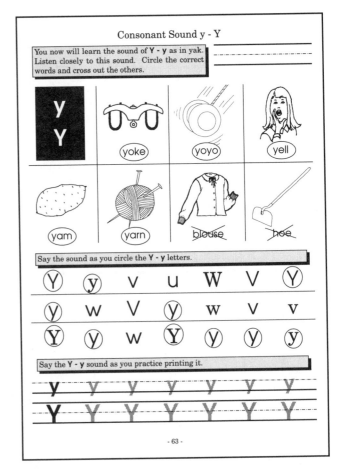

Page 64

Purpose

1. To continue to teach the formation and sound of consonant **y**.
2. To review previously learned consonants and vowels.

Lesson

Quickly drill all the flashcards. If there are any that the student does not know well, separate them for further drilling.

Help the student to spell the following words:

yes   yak   yet   yam   yum   yell

After completing the top exercise on page 64, have the student answer the next section orally before doing the work independently in pencil.

Page 65

Purpose

To teach the sound and formation of **x**.

Before class begins

Open to page 65 and have flashcard **x X** ready.

Lesson

As you show the flashcard, explain that **x** usually comes at the end of words.

Print the following list of words on a board or paper as you ask the student to listen and repeat these words after you pronounce them:

wax   six   mix   tax
box   fix   ax   ox
(even the big word "relax")

Listen to hear if he says the sound as **ks**. Ask him to point to a particular word as you say it. After saying the words several times with him, encourage him to read them alone.

Complete page 65.

Practice printing **x X** on the board or lined paper.

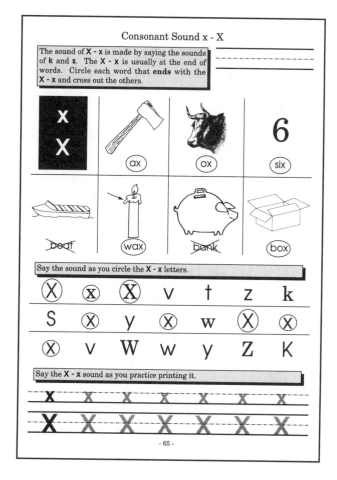

Page 66

Purpose

To review previously learned vowels and consonants.

Lesson

Review by discussing the sound of **x** as it says **ks**.
Quickly drill the other consonants. Help the student to print these words:

ax	tax	wax	fix	six
mix	ox	box	fox	

**Go over page 66. Have the student point to the
correct letters in the lists at the left that make the
beginning sounds in the words that match the
pictures. Then have him do the work in pencil.**

Give extra drill using consonant flashcards. Ask the
student to print on lined paper or the blackboard if
you feel it is necessary.

Page 67

Purpose

To teach the sound and formation of the consonant z.

Before class begins

Open to page 67 and have **z Z** flashcard ready.

Lesson

Show the **z Z** flashcard and say, "This is the last
consonant to learn and it sounds like a bee because
it says **z** as in zig-zag." Ask these questions:

1. Where can we see many wild animals? (**zoo**)
2. What animal looks like a horse with striped pa-
   jamas? (**zebra**)
3. What helps to close up our jacket? (**zipper**)
4. What short man was a tax collector who became
   a Christian? (**Zacchaeus**)
5. What number is a circle? (**zero**)

**Go over page 67. For the exercise at the top of the
page, have the student say the names of the pictures and circle the words that begin with the
sound of "z," as well as coloring their pictures,
and cross out the words that do not. Complete
the rest of the lesson.**

Quickly drill all the flashcards.

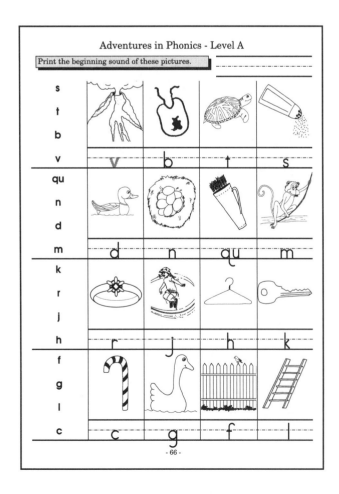

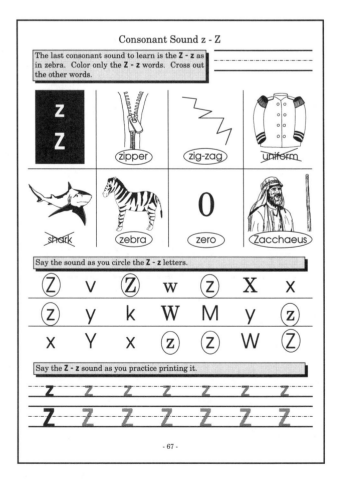

Page 68

Purpose

To reinforce the sound of **z** as well as work with reading many short vowel sound words.

Lesson

Teach the rule that when the sound of **z** comes at the end of words, it is usually doubled as in buzz. Review the **z** sound by having the student print these words:

zap	zip	zig	zag	zest
	fuzz	buzz	fizz	

For page 68, have your student give the answers orally before he prints them with a pencil. For the exercise at the bottom of the page, have the student say the names of the pictures and circle the letter that comes at the *end* of each word.

Page 69

Purpose

To practice reading words with the short vowel **a** sound.

Lesson

With all the previous work with words, the following pages should not be too difficult. Dictate some or all of the following short vowel **a** words for the student to print on the board or lined paper:

had	pat	map	tan	nap
tax	fat	lap	tag	bad

Explain what a *sentence* is to your student. Say, "A sentence is made up of one or more words that tell you something." Teach him that a sentence always begins with a *capital letter* and usually ends with a *period*. Also emphasize the importance of putting a space between each word in a sentence.*

Dictate the following sentence to your student.

Jan and Dan ran fast.

After working the first row with the student, he may be able to complete the rest of page 69 independently.

* Do not be concerned about your child understanding all this new information at once. This will be reinforced in subsequent lessons.

Page 70

Purpose

To practice reading words with the short vowel **e** sound.

Lesson

Ask the student to print the following words on the board or the lined paper:

met   let   beg   fed   hem   wet

Explain what a *sentence* is to your student. Say, "A sentence is made up of one or more words that tell you something." Remind him that a sentence always begins with a *capital letter* and usually ends with a *period*. Also emphasize the importance of putting a space between each word in a sentence.

Dictate the following sentence to your student.

Ted sent Ned ten red pens.

Encourage the student to do page 70 independently.

Page 71

Purpose

To practice reading words with the short vowel **i** sound.

Lesson

Ask the student to print the following words on the board or lined paper:

hit   bit   dig   rip   win   lip

Explain what a *sentence* is to your student. Say, "A sentence is made up of one or more words that tell you something." Remind him that a sentence always begins with a *capital letter* and usually ends with a *period*. Also emphasize the importance of putting a space between each word in a sentence.

Dictate the following sentence to your student.

Jim has six pins in his fist.

The student should be able to do most of page 71 independently.

Page 72

Purpose

To practice reading words with the short vowel **o** sound.

Lesson

Ask the student to print the following words on the board or lined paper:

> n o t   r o b   s t o p   m o p   l o t   o n

Explain that a *sentence* is made up of one or more words that tell you something. Remind him that a sentence always begins with a *capital letter* and usually ends with a *period*. Also emphasize the importance of putting a space between each word in a sentence.

Dictate the following sentence to your student.

> D o n   c a n   h o p   o n   a   b o x .

Encourage the student to do page 72 independently.

Page 73

Purpose

To practice reading words with the short vowel **u** sound.

Lesson

Ask the student to print the following words on the board or lined paper:

> h u m   f u n   t u g   d u g   l u m p

Explain that a *sentence* is made up of one or more words that tell you something. Remind him that a sentence always begins with a *capital letter* and usually ends with a *period*. Also emphasize the importance of putting a space between each word in a sentence.

Dictate the following sentence to your student.

> A   p u p   c a n   j u m p   a n d   r u n .

The student should be able to do most of page 73 independently.

Page 74

Purpose

To encourage independent work in reading and printing.

Lesson

If the student has done well on previous lessons, this one should not be difficult.

Have the student go over this page orally before using a pencil. Have him circle the words first so they can be corrected before he prints them.

Reading

This may be a good time to begin the first lesson in the phonics reader *It is Fun to Read.** However, if you think that your student is not yet ready at this point, you may choose to wait until the lesson on page 84 to begin using this reader.

A couple of days may be needed for the student to grasp each lesson, so do not feel pressured to complete a lesson each day.

Since review is very important in the learning process, you should have your student go over the phonics part of each lesson and read every story three or more times.

---

*This is the first book in the *Christian Liberty Phonics Readers* series. The teacher should first read the introduction to *It is Fun to Read* on the inside front cover, before having the student complete Lesson 1.

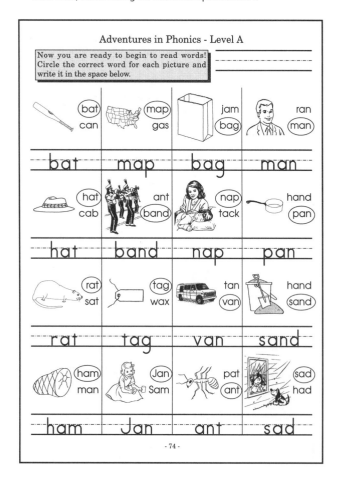

Page 75

Purpose

To give extra practice reading words with the short vowel **a** sound.

Lesson

Before completing page 75, help the student to "warm up" by reading these rhyming words which you may print on the board or paper, or have him read from these directions:

can	bag	bass	fax
fan	rag	gas	tax
man	tag	pass	wax
pan	bat	band	camp
tan	cat	hand	lamp
van	hat	land	stamp

First have your student read the sentence at the top of page 75.* Have him also read the words in the lists at the left, pointing to the pictures they represent. Then he should complete the lesson with a pencil.

---

*The only word that your child may not know is *see*. Help him to pronounce it and encourage him to read the whole sentence.

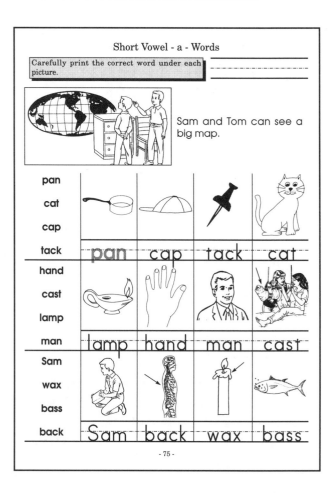

Page 76

Purpose

To give extra practice reading words with the short vowel **e** sound.

Lesson

Print these rhyming short vowel **e** words for the student to read, or ask him to read from these lists:

hen	bell	bed	sent
pen	sell	red	tent
ten	well	Ted	went
jet	best	egg	fed
net	nest	peg	Ned
pet	west	leg	sled

For the first exercise, have your student read each list of words, pointing to the correct word that represents its picture. Then have your student independently do this exercise by circling the correct words; he should change any errors before he prints the answers. Complete the exercise at the bottom of the page.

Page 77

Purpose

To give extra practice reading words with the short vowel **e** sound.

Lesson

Ask your student to read the same short vowel **e** words from the previous lesson.

Can your student read the sentence at the top of page 77?* Encourage him to do this page independently, giving praise and gentle correction when appropriate.

If he is struggling with completing this lesson, have him read the lists of words at the left, while he points to the picture that represents each word. Then have him print the correct answers.

Note that the word "gem" in the second row of the exercise on page 77 uses the soft **g** sound which the student has not yet learned; however, you should encourage him to pronounce it properly and print the word under the correct picture.

*The only words that your child may not know are *see* and *cow*. Help him to pronounce them and encourage him to read the whole sentence.

Page 78

Purpose

To give extra practice reading words with the short vowel **i** sound.

Lesson

Ask the student to read these rhyming words either from this list or from a list you print on the board:

fix	pig	fit	did
mix	wig	mitt	hid
six	twig	sit	lid
fill	gift	pin	king
hill	lift	sin	sing
quill	sift	twin	wing

Check the student's circled answers on page 78 before he prints the correct words.

Page 79

Purpose

To give extra practice reading words with the short vowel **i** sound.

Lesson

Help the student to read these sentences that you may print on the board or lined paper, or have him read from these directions:

Tim has six pigs.

Kim has a big pin.

Jill will fix a quilt.

Jim has a pin in his fist.

Can your student read the sentence at the top of page 79? Encourage him to do this page independently, giving praise and gentle correction when appropriate.

If he is struggling with completing this lesson, have him read the lists of words at the left, while he points to the picture that represents each word. Then have him print the correct answers.

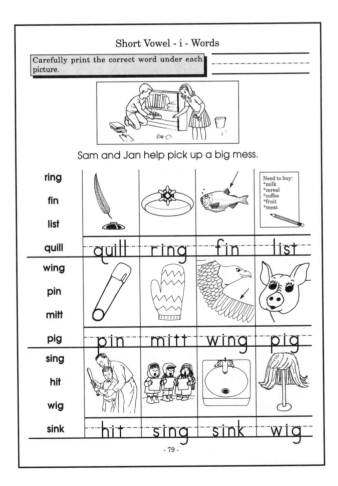

Page 80

Purpose

To give extra practice reading words with the short vowel **o** sound.

Lesson

Help the student to read the following rhyming words either from this list or from a list you print on the board:

hop	cot	block	ox
mop	dot	clock	box
pop	hot	lock	fox
stop	not	rock	lox
top	pot	sock	sox

After your student has circled the correct word next to each picture on page 80, check his answers and have him print the words. Complete the exercise at the bottom of the page.

Page 81

Purpose

To give extra practice reading words with the short vowel **o** sound.

Lesson

Help the student to print or read these sentences:

Tom and Don stop.

A fox hops on a box.

Mom will mop.

A pot is hot.

Can your student read the sentence at the top of page 81?* Encourage him to do this page independently, giving praise and gentle correction when appropriate.

*The only word that your child may not know is *about*. Help him to pronounce it anyway, and have him continue to read the rest of the sentence.

Page 82

Purpose

To give extra practice reading words with the short vowel **u** sound.

Lesson

Help the student to print or read these rhyming words:

up	bun	but	bug
cup	fun	cut	hug
pup	run	hut	jug
sup	sun	nut	mug

After your student has circled the correct word next to each picture on page 82, check his answers and have him print the words.

Page 83

Purpose

To give extra practice reading words with the short vowel **u** sound.

Lesson

Help the student to read or print these sentences:

A pup can jump up on a rug.

Bud will suds the mud on his cuff.

A duck jumps in a tub.

Can your student read the sentence under the image of Wag on page 83? Encourage him to do this page independently, giving praise and gentle correction when appropriate.

Have your student connect the dots to find Wag, if he is able to count up to 31. Otherwise, have him go as far as he can go before you help him complete it. Note that this activity is not required.

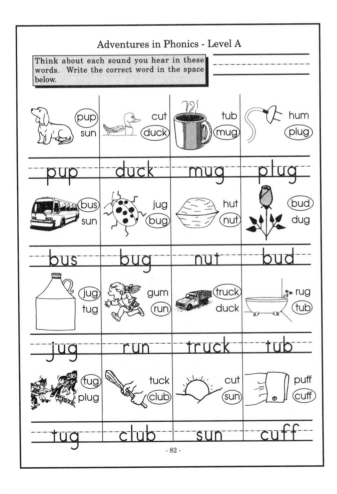

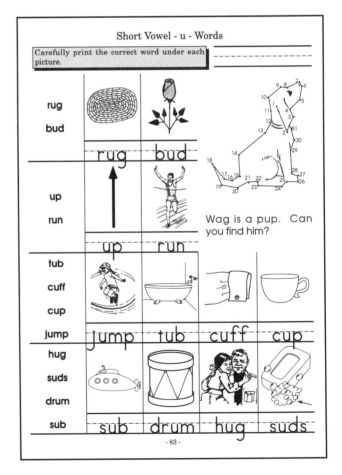

Page 84

Purpose

To review the short vowel **a** words, checking to see if the student can quickly find, circle, and print the correct answers.

Lesson

By way of review, have your student read these sentences and begin studying the words with the short vowel **a** on Chart 1*:

Dan has a cap in his hand.

A cat ran at the rat on a mat.

A man can hand Jan a bag.

If the student is doing well, little, if any, preliminary work needs to be done before he does the work on page 84. For the first exercise, have him circle the correct answers before he prints the words. Then have him complete the page.

Reading

If you have not already done so, this would be a good time to begin reading the first lesson in the primer *It is Fun to Read.*

---

*Chart 1 is found with the set of phonics word charts and flashcards that accompany the student's workbook.

Page 85

Purpose

To provide extra work with short vowel **a** and **e** words, in order to reinforce and confirm the student's ability to read.

Lesson

To prepare for the work on this page, listen as your student reads the words with the short vowel **e** on Chart 2.

For the first exercise on page 85, have your student circle the correct answers before he prints the words. Then have him complete the page.

Reading

It is important to continue using the primer *It Is Fun To Read* during your student's daily studies. A possible lesson may include doing the work connected with the phonics workbook, taking a little break, reviewing the primer story from the previous lesson, and then introducing and reading the next story in the primer.

Having the child read to other family members or friends, as well as to his teacher, helps him to review in an enjoyable way. Plan a little variety in your schedule to help keep your child's interest.

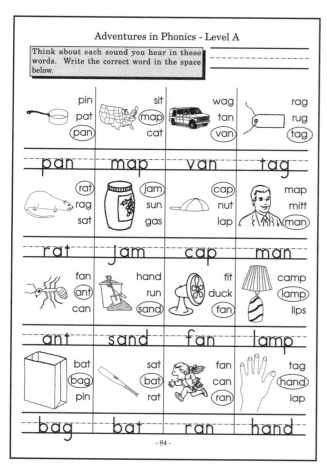

Page 86

Purpose

To review short vowel **a** and **e** words.

Lesson

As a quick review, ask the student to read or print the following sentences:

Sam has a vest and a tan hat.

A man has a pen in his hand.

A hen sat on ten eggs in a nest.

Ted fell on his leg in the jet.

Dan can pet his black cat.

For the first exercise on page 86, have your student circle the correct answers before he prints the words. Then have him complete the page.

Page 87

Purpose

To give extra practice with short vowel **i** words.

Lesson

For a "warm-up" before the workbook page is completed, listen as your student reads the short vowel **i** words on Chart 3. Have it read as many times as you feel necessary.

For the first exercise on page 87, have your student circle the correct answers before he prints the words. Then have him complete the page.

Page 88

Purpose

To give additional work with short vowel **o** words.

Lesson

Begin the lesson by listening as your student reads the short vowel **o** words on Chart 4. Would a second reading help strengthen your student?

For the first exercise on page 88, have your student circle the correct answers before he prints the words. Then have him do the second exercise, tracing the sentences and writing the second and third sentences on the lines below them. Finally, ask your student what the missing picture is in the image at the bottom of the page.

Encourage neat and steady work habits. This page should not take much time to complete.

Page 89

Purpose

To give additional work with short vowel **u** words.

Lesson

Begin the lesson by listening as your student reads the short vowel **u** words on Chart 5.

For the first exercise on page 89, have your student circle the correct answers before he prints the words. Then have him complete the page.

He should be encouraged to work carefully in completing this page. If review is needed, ask the student to answer orally by pointing, before he does the work in pencil.

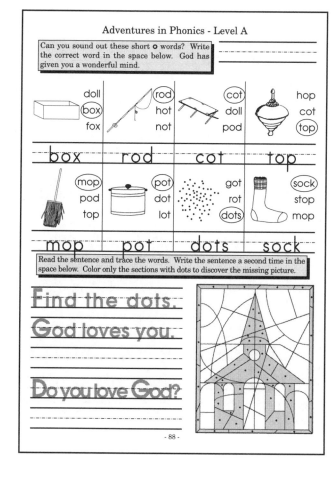

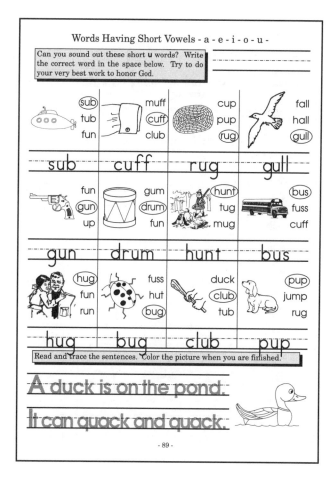

Page 90

Purpose

To teach the marking of short vowels as well as to instruct in copying from a long list.

Lesson

Encourage your student to quickly read the short vowel **a** words on Chart 1.

Discuss the "little smile" or marking that may be used to indicate that the vowel has a short sound. Mention that vowels, unlike most consonants, may make different sounds. These sounds and their markings will be taught in later lessons.

Discuss the directions for page 90 and have your student complete the lesson.

Page 91

Purpose

To give additional work with short vowel marking and printing, encouraging increased independence in completing the page.

Lesson

Listen to your student read the short vowel **e** words on Chart 2.

On the blackboard or paper, print these words and ask him if he remembers and can make the mark that may be put over the vowel to show that it has a short sound:

vest   hand   top   hill   tub

Discuss the directions for page 91 and have your student complete the lesson.

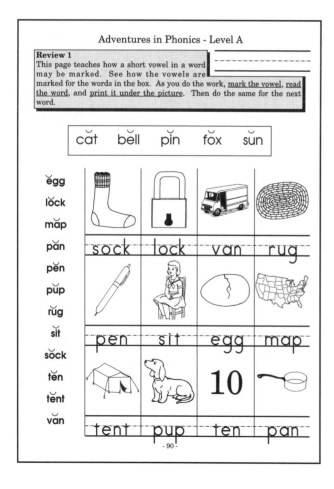

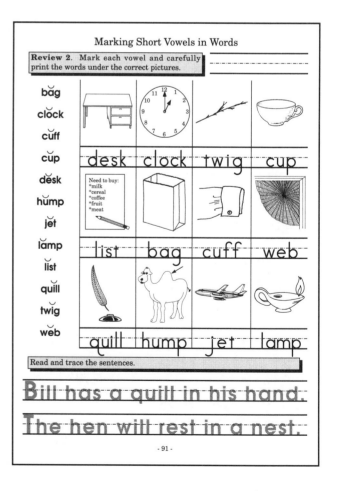

Page 92

Purpose

To give additional work with short vowel words, determining how well the student understands.

Lesson

Listen as your student reads the words with the short vowel **i** on Chart 3.

Discuss the directions for page 92 and have your student complete the lesson.

Page 93

Purpose

To give additional work with short vowel words for the purpose of confirming the student's ability and building his confidence.

Lesson

See how well your student can read the following sentences which you may print on the board or have read from this manual:

The twins ran to get Dad.

Don has spots on his cap.

A red fox ran in the hut.

Listen as he reads the words with the short vowel **o** on Chart 4.

Discuss the directions for page 93 and have your student complete the lesson.

Page 94

Purpose

To give further practice with short vowel words, spelling many of them without a word list from which to copy.

Lesson

As a review, hear your student read the words with the short vowel **u** on Chart 5. Ask him to print these words on the board or a lined paper:

man	bus	pig	sing
cot	cuff	top	well

Discuss the directions for page 94. For Review 5, have your student mark the vowels as he reads the list of words at the left. Then have him point to the correct picture as he reads these same words. Finally, have him print the correct word under each picture and complete the rest of the page.

Page 95

Purpose

To give practice in spelling short vowel words without a word list from which to copy.

Lesson

Your student may think that this is one of his easiest lessons. He does not need to look at a list of words, but just think, as he spells these words. If he has been doing progressively better with reading and spelling words when completing past lessons, he should do well on this page.

Perhaps a little warm-up would be good. After reading the short vowel **a** words on Chart 1, help him to print on the board or lined paper a few of the following words:

gift	lips	gum	box	ten	tag

Before the student begins to write the lesson, ask him to say the vowel sounds he hears in each word (d**u**ck, g**u**m, f**o**x, d**o**ts, etc.).

Have your student print the correct word under each picture on page 95.

Be ready to help if there seems to be a question.

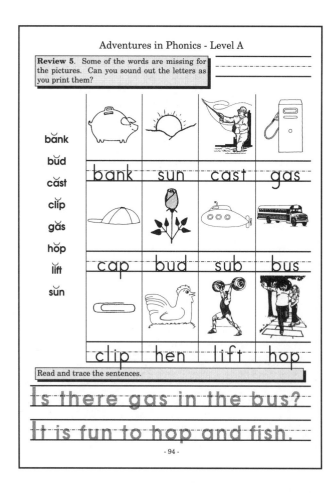

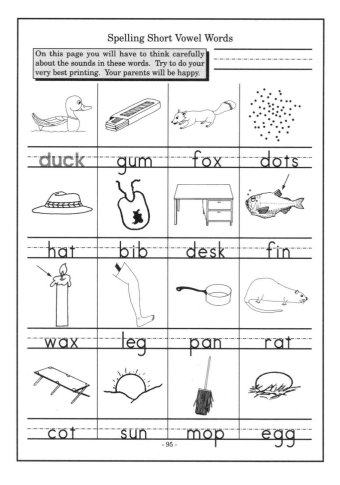

Page 96

Purpose

To give additional practice in spelling vowel words without a word list from which to copy.

Lesson

Evaluate how well your student did on page 95 to determine how much review is needed before doing this page. If the student is uncertain about words, help him print them on the board or lined paper before completing this lesson. Review the short vowel **e** words on Chart 2.

The student may be afraid of making a mistake. Giving your support with gentle correction or praise is always important.

Before the student begins to write the lesson, ask him to say the vowel sounds he hears in each word (m**a**n, c**a**st, p**o**t, t**o**p, etc.)

Complete page 96.

You may also read the question at the bottom of the page and have your child color the picture.

Page 97

Purpose

To continue with additional work in spelling short vowel words.

Lesson

Before this page is written, listen as the student sounds each word. Is the correct vowel being pronounced?

Is any consonant being left out? Are the letters being printed properly? Especially notice the placement of the following letters:

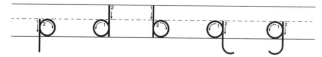

Most of the answers will be written with lower case letters. *Capital letters* are only written at special times, such as the first letter of a proper name (e.g., Adam) and the first letter of the first word in a sentence.

Review the short vowel **i** words on Chart 3.

Have your student print the correct word under each picture on page 97.

You may also read the question at the bottom of the page and have your child color the picture.

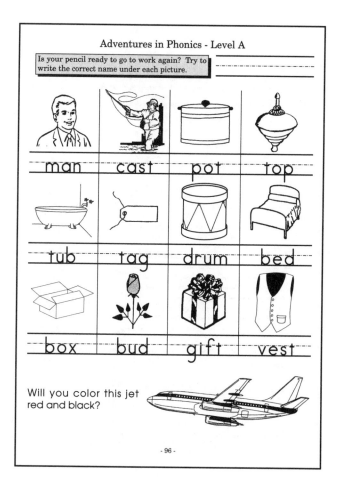

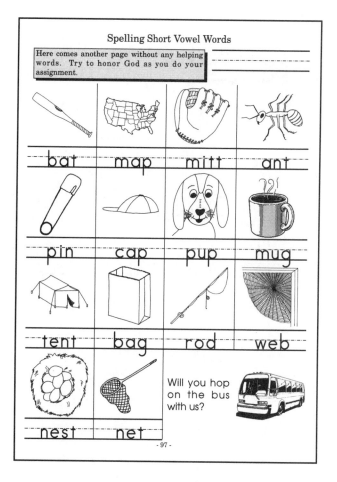

Page 98

Purpose

To again give additional work with spelling short vowel words.

Lesson

Have a quick time of "warm up" as your student reviews the words with the short vowel **o** and **u** on Charts 4 and 5.

Discuss the directions for page 98 and have your student complete the lesson.

When the lesson is completed, look over the work and underline any letters that were the very best ones printed. Ask him to rework some that were not printed as nicely as they should be.

Page 99

Purpose

To introduce words that begin with consonant blends having **l**.

Lesson

There have been a few words beginning with blends in previous lessons, such as **sled** and **block**. Mention that *consonant blends* are two or more consonants that are joined together and their sounds are blended together. Print the following blends on the board or paper and say them having the student repeat after you:

b l	c l	f l	g l	p l	s l
block	clock	flag	glass	plug	sled

Discuss the directions for page 99. After the student is able to pronounce the consonant blends correctly, have him complete the lesson.

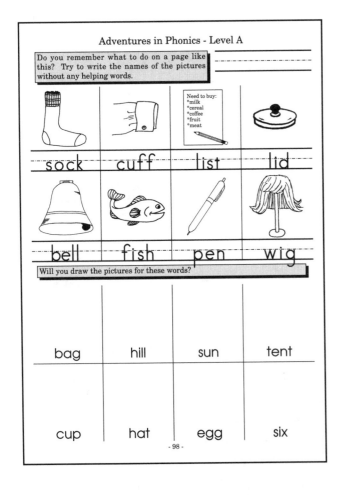

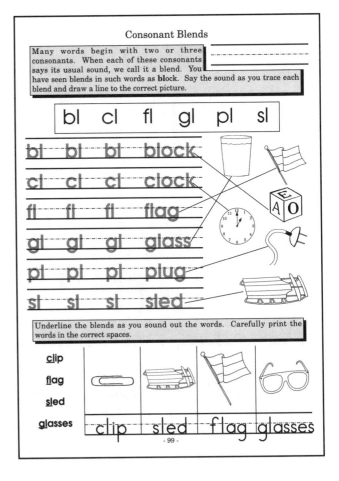

Page 100

Purpose

To introduce words that begin with consonant blends having **r**.

Lesson

Print the following **r** blends on the board or paper, and say them with the student repeating after you many times:

br	**cr**	**dr**	**fr**
brick	crab	drum	frog
gr	**pr**	**tr**	
grass	press	trap	

After your student has learned these blends, go over page 100 orally. After tracing the blends and words in the first exercise, have him draw lines from the words to the correct pictures. Then complete the rest of the lesson.

Reading

This would be a good time to begin the first lesson in the phonics reader *Pets and Pals*.* You should have your student go over the phonics part of the lesson and read the story three or more times.

*This is the second book in the *Christian Liberty Phonics Readers* series. The teacher should first read the introduction to *Pets and Pals* on the inside front cover, before having the student complete Lesson 1.

Page 101

Purpose

To give practice in reading and spelling words beginning with **l** and **r** consonant blends.

Lesson

Quickly review all the flashcards, setting aside any that the student does not know perfectly. Concentrate on these uncertain sounds each day until they are mastered.

Practice saying the first two rows on the Consonant Blends Chart. Watching closely to correct formation in printing letters, help the student to print these words with beginning blends on the board or lined paper:

trip flag crib clap drop plug sled

First have your student read the sentence at the top of page 101. Then discuss the directions for the lesson and have him do the work orally before printing the answers with a pencil.

Encourage him to work independently.

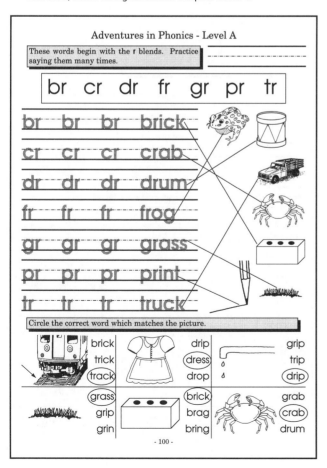

Page 102

Purpose

To introduce words that begin with consonant blends having **s**.

Lesson

Print the followings blends on the board or lined paper and say them as the student repeats them after you many times:

s c	**s k**	**s m**	**s n**
scab	skip	smell	snap
s p	**s t**	**s w**	
spin	steps	swim	

Further drill may be done with the third row of the Consonant Blends Chart.

After your student has learned these blends, go over page 102 orally. After tracing the blends and words in the first exercise, have him draw lines from the words to the correct pictures. Then complete the rest of the lesson.

See if the student can complete the assignment independently.

Page 103

Purpose

To introduce the blends **tw**, **dw**, and **squ**.

Lesson

Practice reading these blends which you may print on the board or paper:

t w	**s q u**	**d w**
twins	squid	dwell

After your student has learned these blends, go over page 103 orally. After tracing the blends and words in the first exercise, have him draw lines from the words to the correct pictures. Then complete the rest of the lesson.

See if the student can complete the assignment independently.

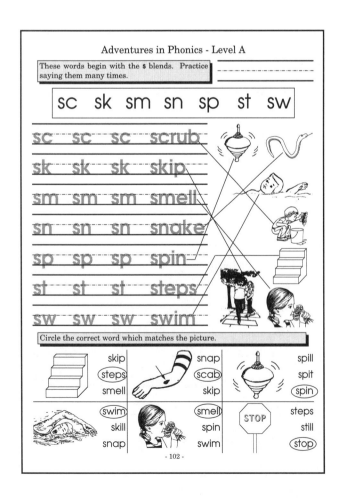

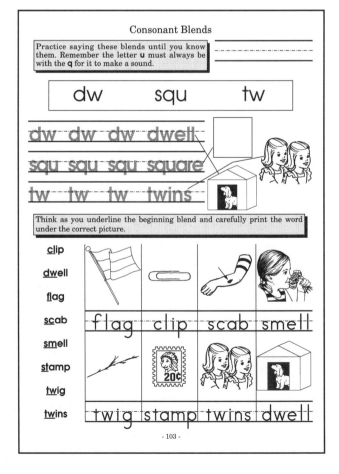

Page 104

Purpose

To introduce words that begin with blends made up of three consonants.

Lesson

Print the following blends on the board or paper, and have the student listen to them and repeat them after you until the blends have been learned:

scr	**spr**	**str**	**spl**
scrub	spring	strap	split

After your student has learned these blends, go over page 104 orally. Have him trace the blends and words in the first exercise and draw lines from the words to the correct pictures. Then complete the rest of the lesson.

At this point you may have had your student complete *It is Fun to Read*. If so, this may be a good time to begin reading the second primer *Pets and Pals*. Each student progresses at a different rate, so do not feel pressured if the first reader is not yet completed. Take as much time as needed so the student has learned the lessons well.

Page 105

Purpose

To review beginning consonant blends.

Lesson

Looking at the Consonant Blends Chart, go over the rows of consonant blends several times to confirm these sounds.

Discuss the directions on page 105. Have your student answer this lesson orally before doing the work in pencil.

Be ready with cheerful compliments or gentle corrections.

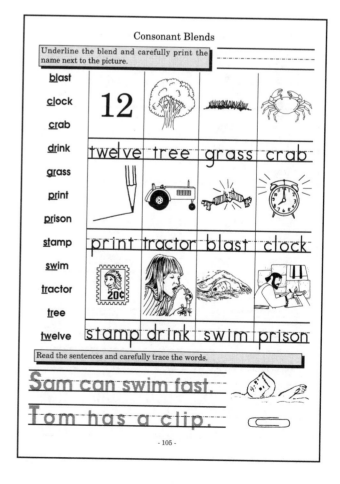

Page 106

Purpose

To introduce an important rule regarding short vowel words that end with **f**, **l**, **s**, and **z**.

Lesson

Previous lessons have included several words that follow this rule:

> When a word has a short vowel sound, usually the ending consonants **f**, **l**, **s**, or **z**, will be doubled.

Print these words and have them read:

cuff	sniff	doll	hill
dress	mitt	buzz	fizz

Discuss the work on page 106 and have the student give the answers orally before he completes the lesson in pencil.

Page 107

Purpose

To review the double consonants **ff**, **ll**, **ss**, and **zz** at the end of short vowel sound words.

Lesson

Print **ff**, **ll**, **ss**, and **zz** on the board or lined paper and help your student to print these words under the correct columns:

ff	ll	ss	zz
puff	still	miss	buzz
cliff	well	fuss	fuzz
stiff	yell	glass	fizz

There are a few words that are exceptions to this rule:

bus   gas   yes   as   is   has   us   his

Discuss the directions on page 107 and have the student give the answers orally before completing the work in pencil.

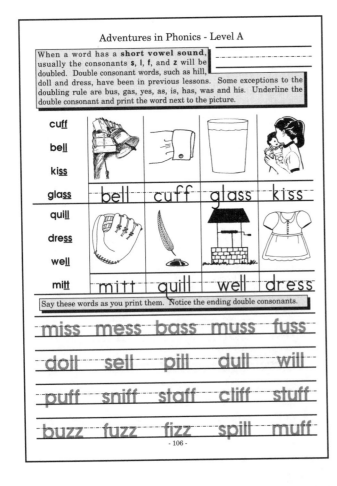

Page 108

Purpose

To review the double ending consonants and to introduce the rule regarding **ck**.

Lesson

In previous lessons, many words have been read that follow this rule:

> When a short vowel sound word ends with a **k** sound, it is spelled with **ck**.

Print these words on the board or lined paper and help the student to read them:

> back   deck   brick   block   duck

Help your student read the **ck** words on Chart 6.

Discuss the directions on page 108. For the first exercise, have your student mark the *short vowels* and underline the *ck*'s in the words at the left and print the correct words under the pictures. Then have him complete the lesson.

Page 109

Purpose

To review short vowel sound words that end with the double letters **ff**, **ll**, **ss**, and **zz** and with the letters **ck**.

Lesson

Print the five sets of ending letters on the board or lined paper and ask the student to print the following words under them:

ff	ll	ss	zz	ck
cuff	fill	pass	fizz	stick
stuff	quill	press	buzz	quack

Have your student read the **ck** words on Chart 6. As time permits during the following lessons, it would be beneficial to review this and any other charts to strengthen him in reading.

Discuss the directions on page 109. For the first exercise, have your student underline the *ending letters* in the words at the left and print the correct words under the pictures. For the second exercise, have him print the correct words under the pictures.

Page 110

Purpose

To introduce short vowel words ending with consonant blends **st**, **sk**, and **sp**.

Lesson

When words end with consonant blends, your student occasionally may not pronounce one of the consonants, or may pronounce the blends incorrectly. Therefore, say each sound for him to hear, as you print the following words:

best	lost	husk	risk	clasp	lisp
fast	rust	mask	task	gasp	wisp

Ask your student to repeat these words with ending consonant blends **st**, **sk**, and **sp**, as you say them again; then have him print them on lined paper.

Discuss the directions on page 110 with your student and have him do the first exercise. For the second exercise, have him read the words and sentences several times before tracing them in the workbook.

Page 111

Purpose

To introduce short vowel words ending with consonant blends **lt**, **lk**, **lp**, **lf**, **mp**, and **nd**.

Lesson

Quickly review the five rows of blends on the Consonant Blends Chart.

To help the student be aware of ending consonants, sound out the following words as you print them on the board or a paper:

tilt	elk	help	self
bump	damp	hand	land

Discuss the directions on page 111. For both exercises, have your student mark the *short vowels* and underline the ending *consonant blends* in the words at the left before printing the correct words under the pictures.

Encourage him to work carefully and neatly, completing the lesson independently.

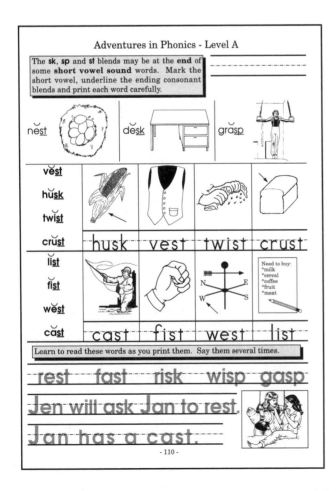

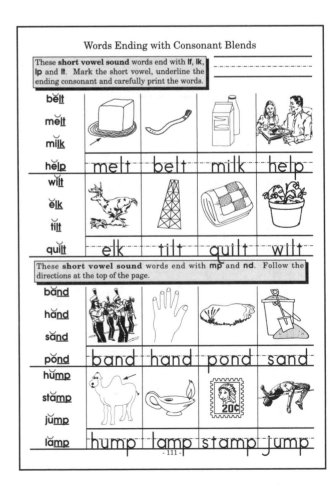

Page 112

Purpose

To introduce short vowel words ending with consonant blends **nt**, **ft**, **pt**, **ct**, or **xt**.

Lesson

If the student is uncertain in pronouncing the consonant blends which have already been learned, quickly drill on the Consonant Blends Chart.

Sound out the following words as you print them, giving special emphasis on the ending consonant blends **nt**, **ft**, **pt**, **ct**, and **xt**:

tent   lift   kept   fact   next

Discuss the directions on page 112 and have your student complete the lesson.

Page 113

Purpose

To give practice in reading words ending with **ng** and **nk**.

Lesson

Print and read the following words to teach or reinforce the **ng** and **nk** sounds. Print them on the board or have the student read from this manual:

sing	wing	ring	bring	sang	stung
sink	pink	mink	link	tank	bank

Discuss the directions on page 113 and have your student complete the lesson.

Page 114

Purpose

To introduce the consonant digraphs **sh** and **ch**.

Before class begins

Have flashcards **ch** and **sh** ready.

Lesson

A *consonant digraph* has two consonants that make one special sound. Print **sh** and **ch** on the board and help your student read the words printed after them.

sh: ship shed shop lash fish

ch: chin chuck chip lunch bench

Continue to teach these digraphs by using the **sh** and **ch** flashcards and the short vowel words in the lists on the back of the Consonant Blends Chart.

Discuss the directions on page 114 and have your student complete the lesson.

Page 115

Purpose

To teach the consonant digraphs **th** and **wh**.

Before class begins

Have flashcards **wh** and **th** ready.

Lesson

Review the flashcards of **sh** and **ch** until the student knows them well. Introduce the consonant digraphs **wh** and **th** by printing them on the board with the following words:

wh: whip when which whiff whisk

The consonant digraph **th** has two sounds, as follows:

    1. **th** may make a hard sound, as in

then this them that mother father

    2. **th** may also make a soft sound, as in

thing think thank bath moth with

Continue to teach these digraphs by using the **th** and **wh** flashcards and the short vowel words in the lists on the back of the Consonant Blends Chart.

Discuss the directions on page 115 and have the student give the answers orally before completing the work in pencil.

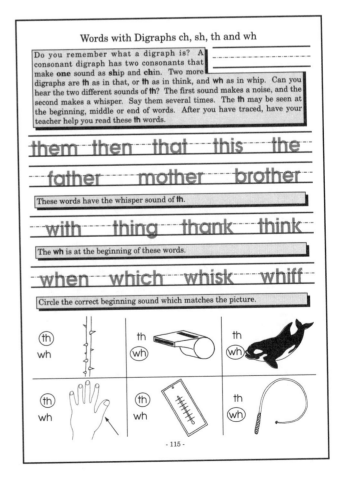

Page 116

Purpose

To introduce the long vowel sound of **a**.

Lesson

Remind the student that when a word has only one vowel in the middle or beginning of a word, it usually has the short vowel sound. Have the student review some of the short vowel words on Charts 1–6.

Today your student will learn a very important rule about what happens when there are two vowels in a word. This *long vowel rule* is as follows:

> When two vowels are in a word, usually the first vowel says its *name*, and the second vowel is *silent*.

Print these words on the board to be read:

can   man   pan   van   ran

When another vowel is added to each word, the vowel **a** now says its *name*. Print these words right under the above words. Read each set many times.

cane   mane   pane   vane   rain

To help in distinguishing between *short* and *long* *vowels*, review the short vowel flashcards and introduce the long vowel flashcards.

Discuss the directions on page 116 and have the student give the answers orally before completing the work in pencil.

Page 117

Purpose

To become better acquainted with the long vowel sound of **a**.

Lesson

Review the short vowel flashcards, mentioning that when one vowel is in a word, it usually has the short vowel sound. Show the long vowel **a** flashcard and say that two vowels are seen in these three sets of letters, which usually follow this rule:

> When two vowels are in a word, usually the first vowel says its *name*, and the second vowel is *silent*.

Print these words on the board for discussion:

cap   mad   hat   pal   tap
cape   made   hate   pale   tape

First have your student read the sentence at the top of page 117. Then discuss the directions on the page and have him give the answers orally before completing the work in pencil.

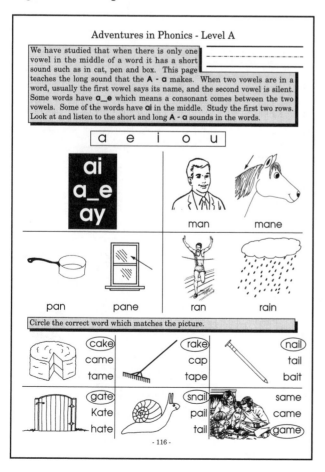

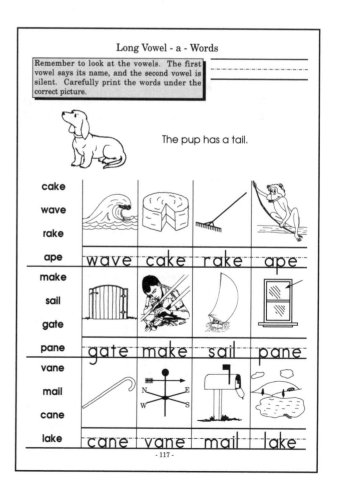

Page 118

Purpose

To give review of the long vowel sound of **a**, with the addition of **ay**.

Lesson

Again review the short vowel flashcards. Then show the long vowel **a** flashcard with two vowels in each set of letters.

It is important to teach the rule that when a **y** is at the end of a word, it is a vowel. When the **y** follows another vowel, the **y** is silent.

Put these words on the board for practice:

bait	tail	cake	date	day	May
pain	vail	cape	game	pray	say

Begin to help your student read the long vowel a words on Chart 7. Continue to review it daily through page 122.

Be patient if the student has a little difficulty. Just do more review and go slower if there is uncertainty.

Discuss page 118 orally before doing any written work.

Page 119

Purpose

To continue giving practice in reading and printing long vowel **a** words.

Lesson

Quickly review the short vowel flashcards to help reinforce these sounds. Also print these words on the board or have them read from this manual:

path   mat   lamp   fan   hand mask
math   fat   stamp   ran   bond task

Show the long vowel **a** flashcard and drill the sound made by these three sets of vowels. Print the following letters and words on the board or a paper and have your student read them:

ai	a_e	ay
pail	name	day
sail	tame	may
tail	same	pay
fail	game	way

On page 119, have your student read the words in the lists at the left and point to the pictures they represent. Then have him print the correct words under the pictures.

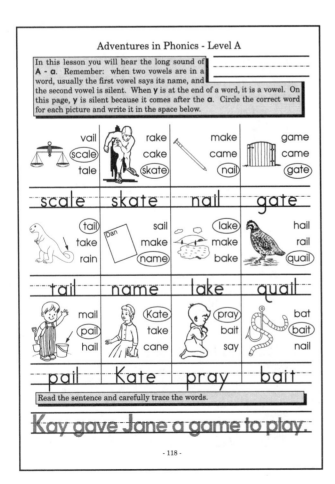

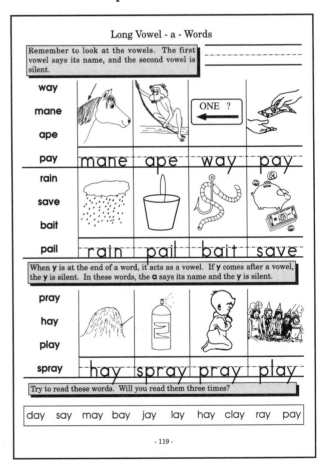

Page 120

Purpose

To teach the marking of vowels in long vowel **a** words and the reading and printing of these words.

Lesson

Quickly drill the short vowel flashcards. Ask the student to read these words:

pat   hand   flat   flash   lamp   clock

tag   band   flag   crash   stamp   lock

Show the long vowel **a** flashcard and discuss the rule it follows, as you look at each set of vowels:

> When two vowels are in a word, usually the first vowel says its *name*, and the second vowel is *silent*.

Help him to read these words:

ai	a_e	ay
rain	late	pray
train	date	play
main	gate	say

Have the student say the long vowel rule as he marks the words above using the following markings:

rāi̸n   lāte̸   prāy̸

Complete page 120.

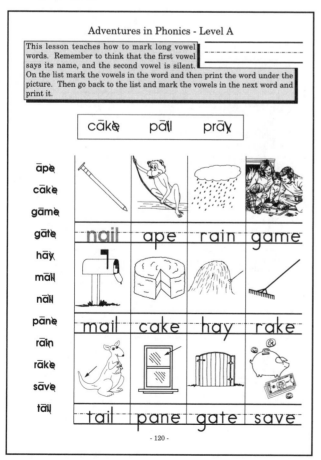

Page 121

Purpose

1. To see if the student can spell long vowel **a** words when only the vowel sets are provided.

2. To introduce the rule regarding **c** and **k**.

Lesson

Several words with **k**, such as **lake** and **cake**, have appeared in recent lessons. The following rules explain when **c** or **k** should be used:

> When **c** is followed by **e**, **i**, or **y**, the **c** says the **s** sound.
>
> When **k** is followed by **e**, **i**, or **y**, the **k** says the **k** sound.

So when we want the **k** sound, we must use **k** to spell words when **e**, **i**, or **y** follow this consonant.

Print these three long vowel **a** sets of letters on the board. Then ask the student to print words under the correct column, as you dictate them:

a_e	ai	ay
tape	pail	hay
lake	sail	pray
ape	nail	tray

Be sure the student knows each picture on page 121. Ask him to sound out and print the correct long vowel *a* words under the pictures, using *a_e*, *ai*, or *ay*. Give help only when necessary.

Page 122

Purpose

To give a last review of long vowel **a** words to help confirm their reading.

Lesson

After a quick drill of the short vowel flashcards, look at and discuss the long vowel **a** flashcard. If more discussion is needed for understanding that sound, look back at the previous long vowel **a** pages for a review.

Complete page 122.

Encourage neat printing, and listen carefully as the words are read.

Reading

This would be a good time to begin the first lesson in the phonics reader *A Time at Home*.* You should have your student go over the phonics part of the lesson and read the story three or more times.

---

*This is the third book in the *Christian Liberty Phonics Readers* series. The teacher should first read the introduction to *A Time at Home* on the inside front cover, before having the student complete Lesson 1.

Page 123

Purpose

To introduce the long vowel sound of **e**.

Lesson

Quickly drill the short vowel flashcards and ask that these words be read.

bed   ten   bet   set   sell   fell

Explain that these words have only one vowel which makes the short sound.

Show the flashcard for the long vowel **e**. The top single **e** follows the following rule:

> When a word has only one vowel which is an **e** at the *end* of the word, it is a long vowel as in **be**, **he**, and **me**.

The other three sets of letters follow the long vowel rule:

> When two vowels are in a word, usually the first vowel says its *name*, and the second vowel is *silent*.

Print the following words under the words (*bed, ten,* etc.) above. Have both sets read several times:

bead   teen   beet   seat   seal   feel

The vowels **ey** follow the long vowel rule and appear in such words as k**ey** and vall**ey**.

Before completing page 123, have the student give answers orally by reading and pointing.

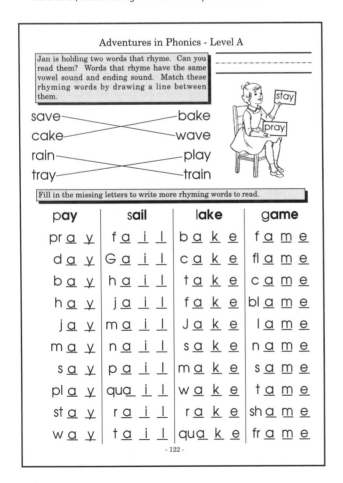

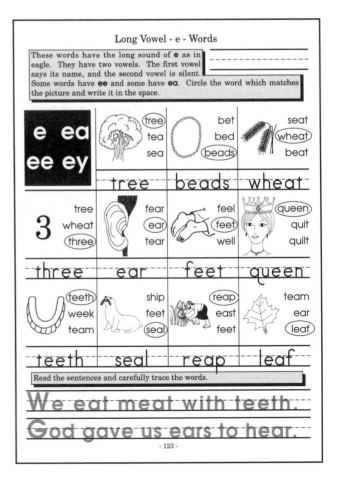

Page 124

Purpose

To give further practice in reading long vowel **e** words.

Lesson

Ask the student to read these words:

ten	pen	egg	tent	hen	bed

peel heel feel eel

feet seat beet heat

bee three teeth tea

Begin to help your student read the words with the long vowel **e** on Chart 8. Continue to daily review this chart through page 128.

On page 124, have your student read the words in the lists at the left and point to the pictures they represent. Then have him print the correct words under the pictures. Then have him complete the rest of the lesson.

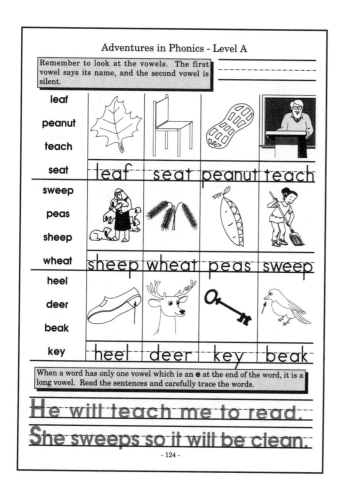

Page 125

Purpose

To teach the marking of long vowels, as well as to reinforce reading long vowel **e** words.

Lesson

Review the short vowel flashcards, mentioning that when one vowel is in a word, it usually has that short vowel sound.

Then drill the long vowel **a** and **e** flashcards, having the student say the name of the vowel for each set seen on the flashcards.

$$ai = \bar{a} \quad a\_e = \bar{a} \quad ay = \bar{a}$$
$$e = \bar{e} \quad ee = \bar{e} \quad ea = \bar{e} \quad ey = \bar{e}$$

Have the student read these words:

cake	rail	tray	name	pain
teeth	meal	bee	leaf	key

Teach the long vowel marking and say the rule each time as the student marks the words above as follows:

tēeth   mēal   kēy

Ask the student to read the list of words on page 125 before doing the work.

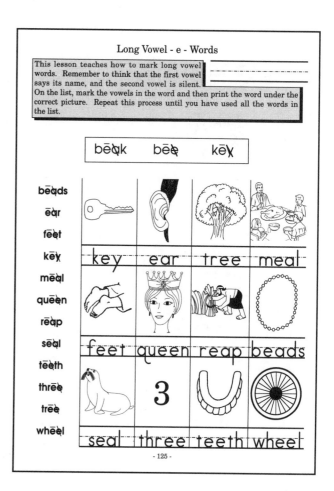

Page 126

Purpose

To see if the student can spell long vowel **e** words when only the vowel sets are provided.

Lesson

Print the following two sets of vowels on the board or paper and ask your student to print the words, as you dictate them, under the correct column:

ea	ee
ear	deep
peas	feet
leaf	tree
seat	steel
teach	queen

Be sure the student knows each picture on page 126. Ask him to sound out and print the correct words under the pictures, using *ea* or *ee*. Print the correct words under the pictures at the bottom of the page.

Give help only when necessary.

Page 127

Purpose

To review long vowel **a** and **e** words.

Lesson

Quickly drill the short vowel flashcards. Then discuss the two long vowel flashcards **a** and **e**.

Ask the student to read the words in the lists at the left on page 127 and have him answer orally before doing the work in pencil.

Remember to continue to read the words with the long vowel **e** on Chart 8.

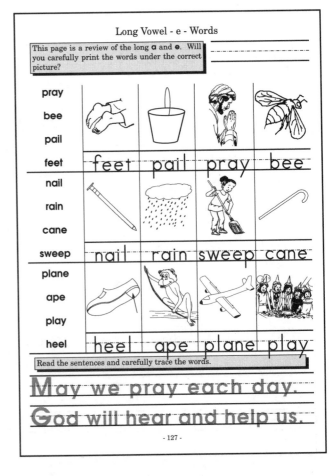

Page 128

Purpose

1. To review long vowel **e** words

2. To introduce the long **a** vowel sound spelled with **ey**, as in **they** and **obey**.

Lesson

After a quick drill with short vowel flashcards, review the two long vowel flashcards.

Carefully discuss page 128, asking the student to answer orally before doing the work in pencil.

Page 129

Purpose

To introduce the long vowel sound of **i**.

Lesson

Quickly review the short vowel flashcards.

Print these words for the student to read:

pin   kit   bit   rid   Tim   hid

Show the long vowel **i** flashcard and discuss the long vowel rule for the two top sets of of vowels—**i_e**, as in **line**, and **ie** as in **tie**. Remember the rule:

> When two vowels are in a word, usually the first vowel says its *name*, and the second vowel is *silent*.

Print these words under the above words and have your student read the sets many times:

pine   kite   bite   ride   time   hide

In previous lessons, the rule about **y** being a vowel at the end of a word has been taught. In this lesson, however, the **y** is the only vowel in the word so it has the long **i** sound, as in **sky** and **fly**.

Carefully discuss page 129, asking the student to answer orally before doing the work in pencil.

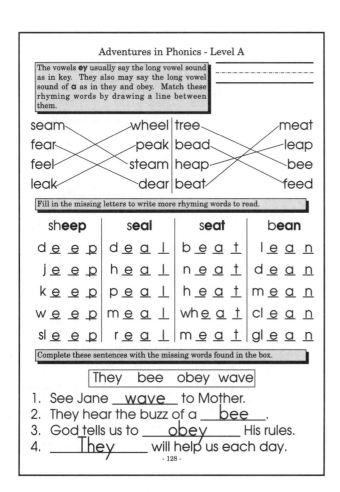

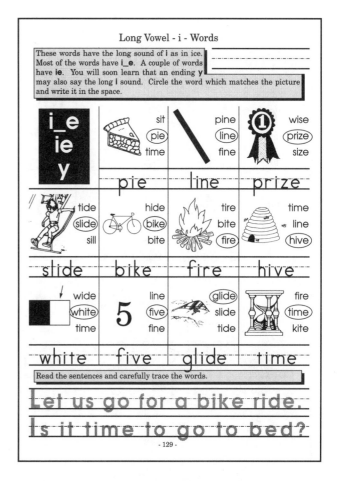

Page 130

Purpose

To practice reading long vowel **i** words.

Lesson

Ask the student to read these words:

bit	dim	slid	fin	win	pin
bite	dime	slide	fine	wine	pine

There are a few words that are spelled like long vowel words, but the first vowel does **not** say its name; it makes the short vowel sound. These short vowel words, which end with the sound of the consonant **v**, usually are spelled with a silent **e**. Read the following short vowel words a couple of times:

gĭve   lĭve   hăve

Begin to help your student read the words with the long vowel **i** on Chart 9. Continue to daily review this chart through page 133.

Carefully discuss page 130, asking the student to answer orally before doing the work in pencil.

Page 131

Purpose

To teach the marking of long vowels, as well as to reinforce reading long vowel **i** words.

Lesson

Review the short vowel flashcards, mentioning that when one vowel is in a word, it usually has these short vowel sounds.

Next, drill the three long vowel flashcards, paying special notice to the long vowel **i** sets.

Teach the long vowel marking and say the rule each time as the student marks these words that you have written on the board:

līne   hīke   pīe   nīne   bīte   tīe

Carefully discuss page 131, asking the student to answer orally before doing the work in pencil.

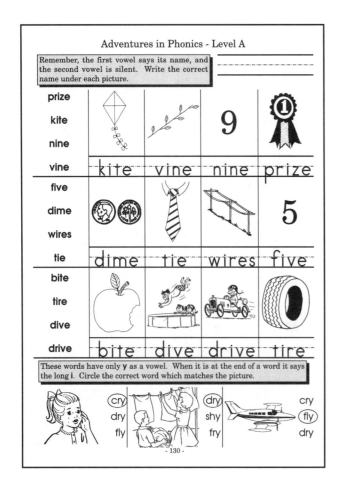

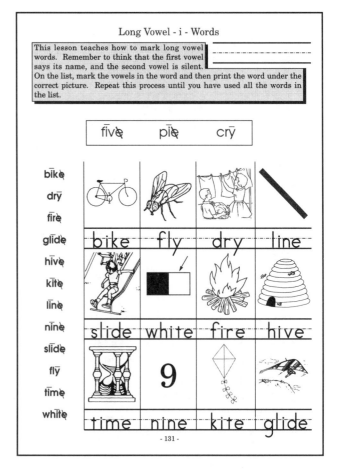

Page 132

Purpose

To see if the student can spell long vowel **i** words with only the vowel sets provided.

Lesson

Print these two sets of vowels on the board and ask the student to print the correct words, as you dictate them, under the correct column.

i_e	y
line	fly
dime	dry
tire	cry
slide	sky
prize	fry

Be sure the student knows each picture on page 132. Ask him to sound out and print the words under *i_e* and *y*. Print the correct words under the pictures at the bottom of the page.

Page 133

Purpose

To review more long vowel **i** words, emphasizing the long vowel rule.

Lesson

Print several examples on the board to show what change takes place in vowel sounds when a second vowel is in a word:

rip	rid	Tim	kit	can	at
ripe	ride	time	kite	cane	ate

Show the long vowel **i** flashcard and discuss the long vowel rule:

> When two vowels are in a word, usually the first vowel says its *name*, and the second vowel is *silent*.

Explain that rhyming words have the same vowel sounds and the same ending sounds as in **time** and **lime**. Ask the student to read these rhyming words:

fly	file	bike	pine	fire
try	tile	hike	line	hire
fry	mile	Mike	vine	tire
cry	smile	like	dine	wire

On page 133, the student should answer orally before printing the work.

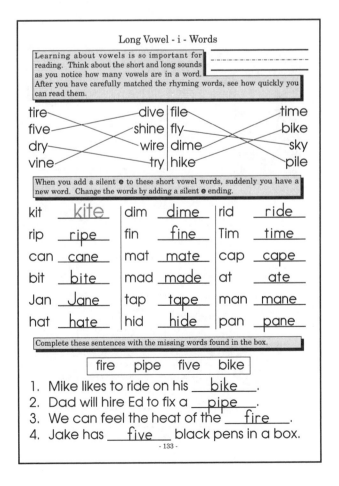

Page 134

Purpose
To introduce the long vowel sound of **o**.

Lesson
Quickly drill the short vowel flashcards with emphasis on the short sound of **o**. Ask the student to read these words several times:

hop   got   rob   not   rod   cot

Teach that when a second vowel is added to these words, the letter **o** will say its name, as in **oak**. Print these words under the above line, and have them read many times:

hope   goat   robe   note   road   coat

Show the flashcard for the long vowel **o**. The top single **o** follows this rule:

When a word has only one vowel which is an **o** at the *end* of the word, it is a long vowel as in **no** and **so**.

The other four sets of letters follow the long vowel rule. Note that the letter **w** acts like a vowel when it follows another vowel. Do you remember the rule?

When two vowels are in a word, usually the first vowel says its *name*, and the second vowel is *silent*.

Ask the student to circle the answers for the first exercise on page 134 before writing them in pencil. Then have him complete the second exercise.

Page 135

Purpose
To give further practice in reading and printing long vowel **o** words.

Lesson
Quickly drill the short vowel flashcards followed by the long vowel flashcards. Then review the long vowel rule:

When two vowels are in a word, usually the first vowel says its *name*, and the second vowel is *silent*.

Help your student to read the words with the long vowel **o** on Chart 10. Continue to have this chart read daily through page 138.

Ask the student to read the words in the lists at the left on page 135, pointing to the correct pictures that these words represent. Then have him complete the lesson in pencil.

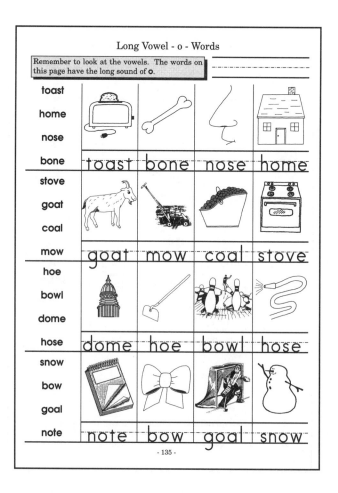

Page 136

Purpose

To teach how to mark long vowel **o** words.

Lesson

On the board or paper, print the following sets of letters which make the long vowel **o** sound, dividing them into columns. Ask the student to spell each word as you dictate it, telling him the correct column in which it goes:

oa	o_e	ow
coat	home	slow
toast	rope	blow
road	note	glow

Have the student mark the vowels in the words he has written above. Each time he marks the vowels, have him say the following long vowel rule:

When two vowels are in a word, usually the first vowel says its *name*, and the second vowel is *silent*.

cōa̸t   hōmė̸   slōw̸

tōa̸st   rōpė̸   blōw̸

rōa̸d   nōtė̸   glōw̸

Carefully discuss page 136, asking the student to answer orally before doing the work in pencil.

Page 137

Purpose

To see if the student can spell long vowel **o** words with only the vowel sets provided.

Lesson

Drill the long vowel flashcards.

On the board or paper, print the following sets of letters at the top of the three columns. Ask the student to spell each word as you dictate it, telling him the correct column in which it goes. Mention that the long vowel words have two vowels, and the short vowel words have one vowel.

o_e	oa	o
yoke	boat	box
pole	coal	dots
bone	toad	sock
rope	toast	rod

Be sure the student knows each picture on page 137. Ask him to sound out and print the words under o_e* and oa. Print the correct words under the pictures at the bottom of the page.

*Explain to your student that the word *nose* in the first exercise on page 137 has the letter s which makes the "z" sound.

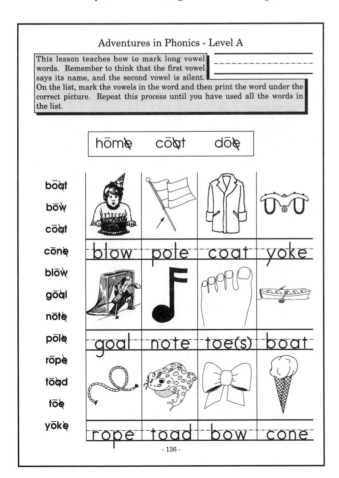

Page 138

Purpose

To practice reading more long vowel **o** words.

Lesson

Quickly drill the short vowel flashcards and the four long vowel flashcards. If the student is a bit uncertain, look back on a lesson that may help in review. Have these rhyming words read:

toad	nose*	row	foam
road	pose	low	home
load	rose	show	dome

Discuss the directions carefully and have the student answer orally whatever may be appropriate before completing the work in pencil. Is the student able to read the words with ease?

---

*Explain to your student that the words *nose, pose,* and *rose* in the table above has the letter **s** which makes the "z" sound. This is also true for the middle list of words in the second exercise on page 138 of the workbook.

Page 139

Purpose

To introduce the long vowel sound of **u**.

Lesson

Quickly review the short vowel flashcards, putting special attention on the short sound of **u**. Print the following words on the board and mention that they have only one vowel:

fuss   cub   tub

As you print a second group of words under the first group, explain that these words have another vowel added at the end. This makes the first vowel say the long sound of **u** which may sound like its name (**yu**) or have the sound of **u** as in **suit**.

fuse   cube   tube

After the student reads these words many times, show the flashcard for the long vowel **u**, and discuss the first two sets with two vowels. Then explain that the same sound is made by **ew** as in **new**.

Carefully go over page 139 orally before the answers are printed.

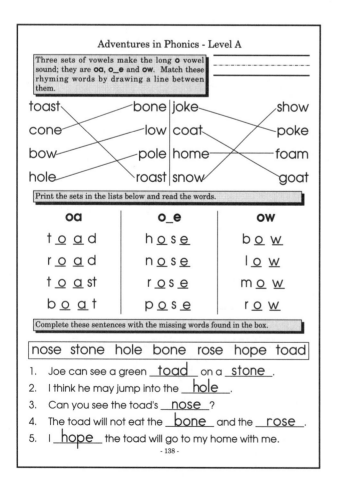

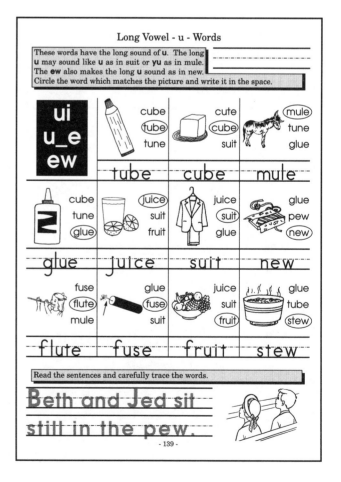

Page 140

Purpose

To give further practice in reading words with the long vowel sound of **u**.

Lesson

If there seems to be any uncertainty about the sounds the consonants or short vowels make, be sure to continue to teach and reinforce them daily by reviewing the flashcards and previous lessons.

Help your student to read the words with the long vowel **u** on Chart 11. This chart should be read each day through page 143.

Ask the student to read the words in the lists at the left on page 140, pointing to the correct pictures that these words represent. Then have him complete the lesson in pencil.

Page 141

Purpose

To teach the marking of vowels in long vowel **u** words.

Lesson

Review the short vowel flashcards, mentioning that usually only one vowel is in the word when the vowel has the short sound.

Drill the long vowel flashcards after saying that usually two vowels are in a word when the first vowel says its name.

Print the following words on the board and show how the vowels should be marked, saying the rule:

> When two vowels are in a word, usually the first vowel says its *name*, and the second vowel is *silent*.
>
> tūne   flūte   frūit   sūit

For the **ew** sound, just underline the ew.

> m<u>ew</u>   st<u>ew</u>   bl<u>ew</u>   dr<u>ew</u>   ch<u>ew</u>

Help the student read the list of words at the left on page 141 before writing the work in pencil.

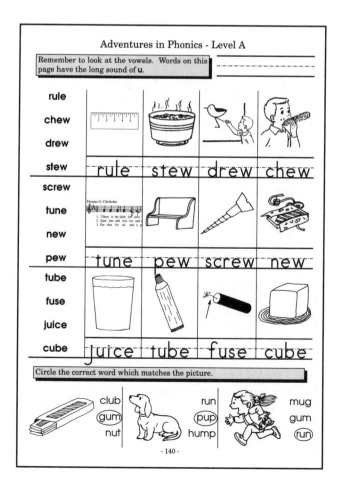

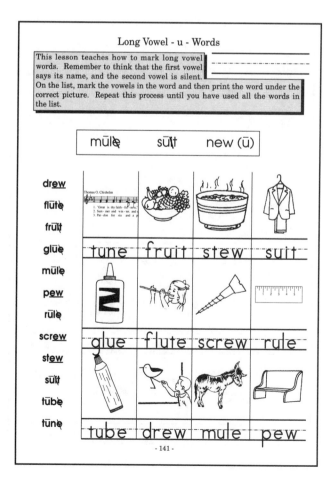

Page 142

Purpose

To give additional review in reading and printing words with the long vowel **u**.

Lesson

Review the long vowel rule:

> When two vowels are in a word, usually the first vowel says its *name*, and the second vowel is *silent*.

Ask the student to read these words and sentences:

new   fruit   glue   cube   rule

chew   suit   blue   tube   mule

Luke plays a tune on his new flute.

June has a new blue suit.

Sue likes to eat stew.

Ask the student to read the sentence next to the blue suit at the top of page 142. Then have him read the words in the lists at the left, pointing to the correct pictures that these words represent. Finally, have him complete the lesson in pencil.

Page 143

Purpose

To give another review of long vowel **u** words.

Lesson

If the student has difficulty with any consonant or vowel, spend as much time as you feel is necessary with those particular flashcards. Look back on completed pages for help with specific words.

Review the long vowel rule as you look at the following words: cūte sūɪt.

> When two vowels are in a word, usually the first vowel says its *name*, and the second vowel is *silent*.

Discuss page 143, and after completing the written work, go over it several times.

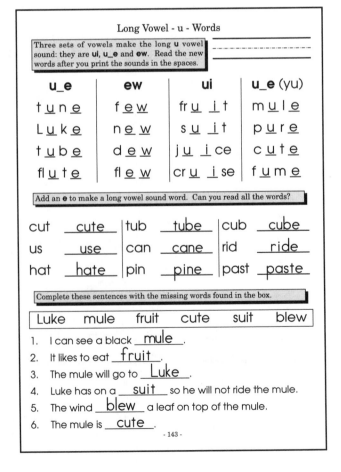

Page 144

Purpose

To review words with long vowels **i**, **o**, and **u**.

Lesson

Ask the student to read these words, noting that the short vowel words usually have only one vowel, and the long vowel words usually have two vowels:

not	⇨ note	rid	⇨ ride
cub	⇨ cube	us	⇨ use
bit	⇨ bite	pin	⇨ pine
cot	⇨ coat	tub	⇨ tube
kit	⇨ kite	rob	⇨ robe
cut	⇨ cute	dim	⇨ dime
hop	⇨ hope	rod	⇨ rode
fuss	⇨ fuse	rip	⇨ ripe

Complete page 144.

Page 145

Purpose

To use this page as an informal test of the student's ability to read long vowel words.

Lesson

To introduce the lesson, print the following sets of vowels on the board and ask the student to print words in the correct columns, as you dictate:

a_e	ee	i_e	o_e	u_e
game	deer	tire	smoke	fuse
vase	feet	slide	home	mule
cape	jeep	fine	pole	tune
tame	sheep	wire	yoke	cube

Ask the student to mark the vowels in the first word of each column.

gāme | dēer | tīre | smōke | fūse

Complete page 145.

For the next nine pages of long vowel review, spend time helping your student recite some of the long vowel charts which you think would be helpful.

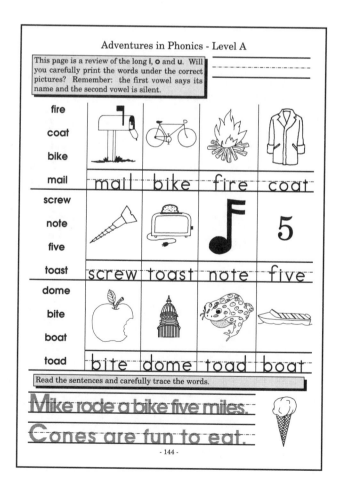

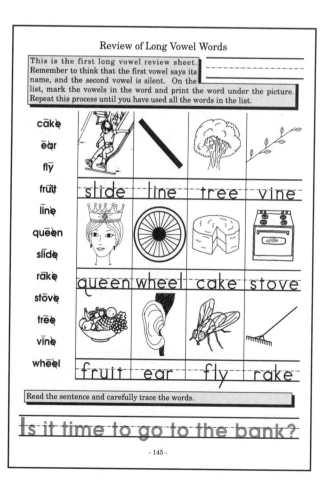

Page 146

Purpose

1. To review long vowel words, checking the student's ability to read and work independently.

2. To briefly review short vowel **a** words.

Lesson

Print the following sets of vowels on the board. Ask the student to print the words in the correct columns, as you dictate:

ai	ea	ie	oa	ui
trail	treat	tie	boat	suit
fail	mean	lie	toad	fruit
paint	beast	pie	coal	juice

Ask the student to mark the vowels in the first word of each column.

After discussing the lesson, listen as your student reads the list of words at the left on page 146 before he completes the page.

Can you and the student see improvement in his reading and printing abilities? Give special recognition and commendation.

Help the student recite one or more of Charts 7–12. Especially focus on Chart 12 for **Long Vowel Rule 2.**

Page 147

Purpose

1. To give further review of long vowel words.

2. To briefly review short vowel **u** words.

Lesson

Review the long vowel rule as you look at the following words:

tail   read   time   tow   blue

When two vowels are in a word, usually the first vowel says its *name*, and the second vowel is *silent*.

Ask the student to read these rhyming words:

drew	bow	mail	fire	beet
flew	slow	nail	hire	feet
stew	show	pail	tire	meet
threw	snow	sail	wire	sheet

Complete page 147.

Help the student recite one or more of Charts 7–12.

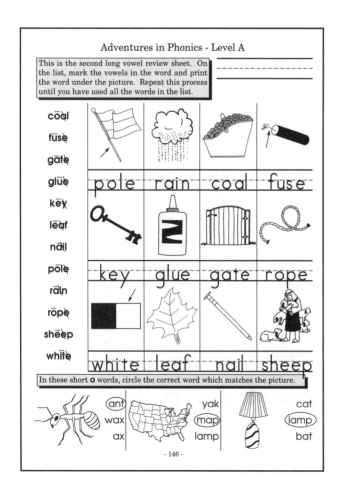

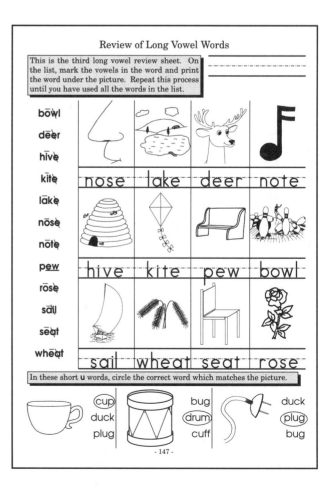

Page 148

Purpose

1. To give additional review to help build confidence in reading long vowel words.

2. To briefly review short vowel **e** words.

Lesson

Print the following sets of vowels on the board. Ask the student to print the words in the correct columns, as you dictate:

ay	ow	y	ee	u_e
tray	blow	sky	cheer	flute
clay	throw	fly	steer	rule
gray	slow	shy	teeth	cube

Complete page 148.

Help the student recite one or more of Charts 7–12. Especially focus on Chart 12 for **Long Vowel Rule 2**.

Page 149

Purpose

1. To give a final review of printing long vowel words with a list provided.

2. To briefly review short vowel **o** words.

Lesson

By way of review, go over the Consonant Blends and Digraphs Chart several times.

Ask the student to say the long vowel rule:

> When two vowels are in a word, usually the first vowel says its **name**, and the second vowel is **silent**.

As he recites the rule, have him mark these words:

> hope   paint   shine   wheat   true

Complete page 149.

Help the student recite one or more of Charts 7–12.

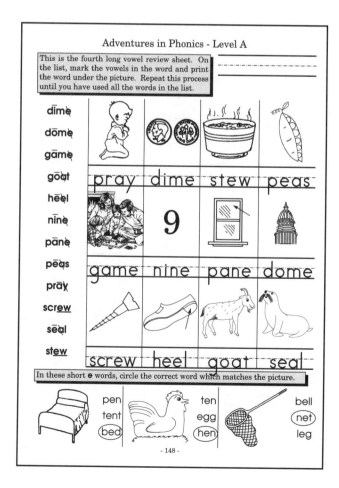

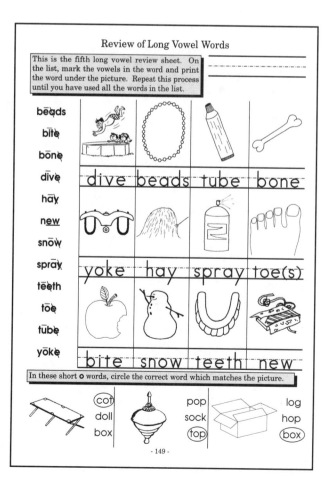

Page 150

Purpose

1. To give practice in spelling long vowel words with only the vowel sets provided.
2. To briefly review short vowel **i** words.

Lesson

Print the following sets of vowels on the board. Ask the student to print the following words in the correct columns, as you dictate:

a_e	ee	i_e	o_e	u_e
bake	deep	fire	home	fuse
cave	sleep	five	poke	rule
tame	weep	wire	stole	tune

Discuss the rules regarding the use of **k** or **c** before the vowels **e**, **i**, or **y**.

When **c** is followed by **e**, **i**, or **y**, the **c** says the **s** sound.

When **k** is followed by **e**, **i**, or **y**, the **k** says the **k** sound.

So when we want the **k** sound, we must use **k** to spell words when **e**, **i**, or **y** follow this consonant.

For the first exercise on page 150, have the student print the correct words under *a_e*, *ee*, *i_e*, *o_e*, and *u_e*. For the second exercise, have him circle the correct words that match the pictures.

Help the student recite one or more of Charts 7–12.

Page 151

Purpose

1. To give further practice in spelling long vowel words with only the vowel sets provided.
2. To briefly review short vowel **i** words.

Lesson

Print the following sets of vowels on the board. Ask the student to print the following words in the correct columns, as you dictate:

ai	oa	ui	ay	ea
chain	float	fruit	clay	fear
main	loan	juice	pray	heat
wait	roast	suit	stay	leaf

For the first exercise on page 151, have the student print the correct words under *ai*, *oa*, *ui*, *ay*, and *ea*. For the second exercise, have him circle the correct words that match the pictures.

Encourage neat printing.

Help the student recite one or more of Charts 7–12.

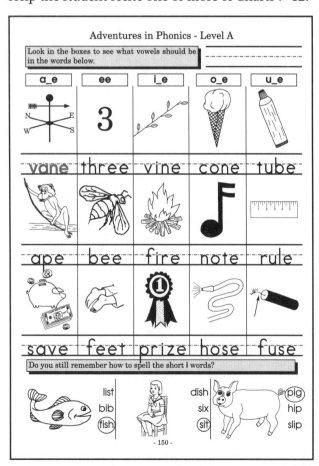

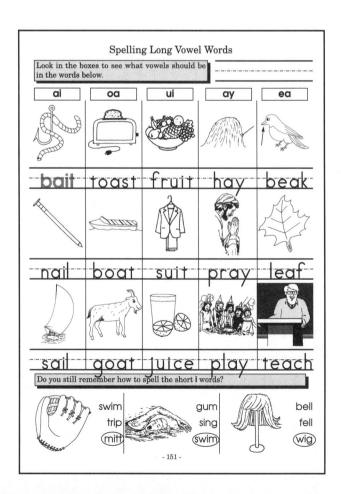

Page 152

Purpose

1. To have additional practice in spelling long vowel words with only the vowel sets provided.
2. To briefly review long vowel **ow** words.

Lesson

Print the following sets of vowels on the board. Ask the student to print the following words in the correct columns, as you dictate:

o a	e a	a y	y	e w
throat	seam	tray	fly	drew
groan	tea	hay	dry	flew
roam	dear	jay	shy	grew

Be sure the student knows each of the pictures on page 152 before he completes the lesson.

Help the student recite one or more of Charts 7–12. Especially focus on Chart 12 for **Long Vowel Rule 2.**

Page 153

Purpose

To teach the rule that a single **i** usually is short except when followed by **ld**, **nd**, and **gh**. Note that the **gh** is silent.

Lesson

Ask the student to practice reading the following rhyming words before studying the first half of Chart 13 with long vowel **i** words:

wild	find	light
child	bind	sight
mild	grind	might

Ask the student to read the words in the lists at the left on page 153 and print the correct words under the pictures. Then have him read and trace the words at the bottom of the page.

Help the student recite one or more of Charts 7–12. Especially focus on Chart 13 for **Long Vowel Rule 3.**

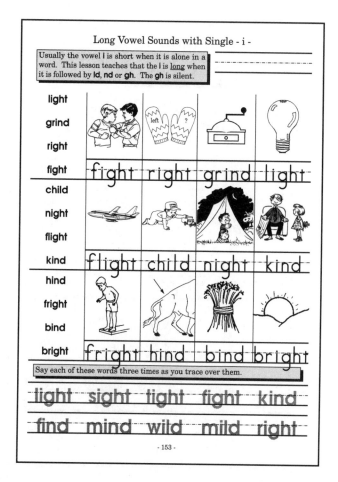

Page 154

Purpose

1. To teach the rule that a single **o** may have the long vowel sound when it has two consonants after it, as with **old**, **oll**, **olt**, **ost**, and **oth**.

2. To review beginning consonant blends.

Lesson

Ask the student to practice reading the following rhyming words before studying the second half of Chart 13 with long vowel **o** words:

old	host	roll	bolt	both
fold	most	toll	colt	
told	post	stroll	molt	

Ask the student to read the words in the lists at the left on page 154 and print the correct words under the pictures. Then have him complete the exercise at the bottom of the page.

On the board or paper, have the student print the long **o** words in the box at the bottom of page 154, as he recites them.

Help the student recite one or more of Charts 7–12. Especially focus on Chart 13 for **Long Vowel Rule 3**.

Page 155

Purpose

To introduce the sound of **ow** and **ou** as in the words **cow** and **house**.

Lesson

If there is any uncertainty about previous flash-cards, drill as much as necessary.

Show the **ow ou** flashcard and teach their sound. The **ow** has already been taught as having the long **o** sound. Mention that the **ou** makes many other sounds, but this lesson teaches the **ou** as in h**ou**se.

Ask the student to practice reading the following rhyming words:

owl	house	ouch	towel
howl	mouse	pouch	vowel
fowl	blouse	couch	

Ask the student to read the words in the lists at the left on page 155 and print the correct words under the pictures. Then have him complete the exercise at the bottom of the page.

Help him recite the **ow ou** words on Chart 14.

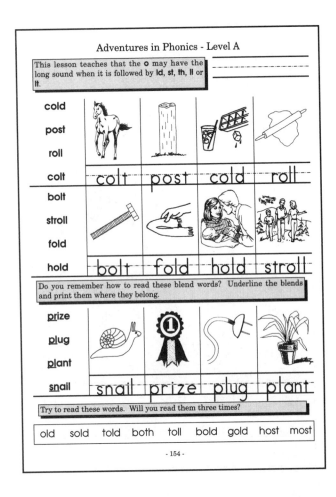

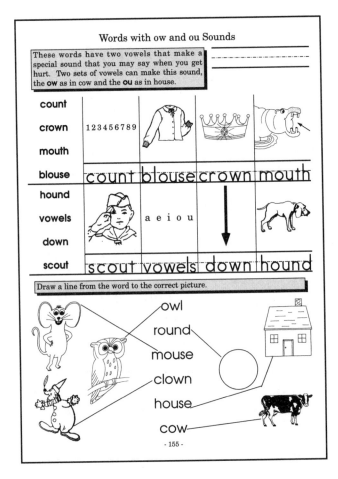

Page 156

Purpose

1. To give further review in reading and printing **ow ou** words.

2. To give a brief review of short vowel **i** words.

Lesson

Ask the student to practice reading the following rhyming words:

bound	cower	clown
found	flower	crown
ground	power	down
pound	plower	drown
round	tower	frown
sound	shower	town

Ask the student to read the words in the lists at the left on page 156 and print the correct words under the pictures. Then have him complete the exercises at the bottom of the page.

Help him recite the **ow ou** words on Chart 14.

Page 157

Purpose

To practice reading and printing the **ow ou** sound.

Lesson

Ask the student to practice reading the following rhyming words:

brown	growl	ouch	how
crown	howl	couch	now
frown	owl	pouch	cow

Complete page 157.

As words are getting longer and the spaces may be a bit small, teach how to form slender letters.

Help him recite the **ow ou** words on Chart 14.

Reading

This would be a good time to begin the first lesson in the phonics reader *It is a Joy to Learn.** You should have your student go over the phonics part of the lesson and read the story three or more times.

---

*This is the fourth book in the *Christian Liberty Phonics Readers* series. The teacher should first read the introduction to *It is a Joy to Learn* on the inside front cover, before having the student complete Lesson 1.

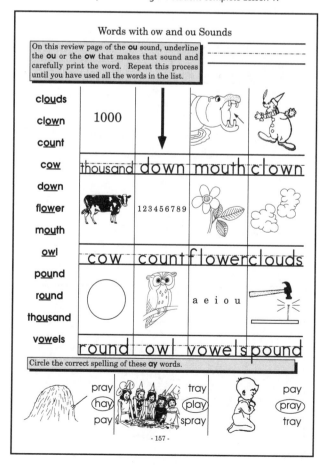

Page 158

Purpose

To introduce the sound of **är**, as in **car**.

Lesson

Tell the student that the consonant **r** may make the vowels have different sounds than the short or long vowel sounds. Show the flashcard for **är** and teach the sound. Show the marking over the **ä**. Have this list of rhyming words read several times and ask that the marking be placed over the **a**:

car	arm	card	art
far	alarm	hard	cart
jar	farm	lard	chart
star	harm	yard	dart

Complete page 158.

Help him recite the **är** words on Chart 15.

Page 159

Purpose

To review the sound of **är**.

Lesson

After drilling the **ow ou** and **är** flashcards, ask the student to print the following rhyming words on the board:

art	far	arm	ark	card
part	jar	farm	bark	hard
tart	star	harm	dark	yard

Complete page 159.

Help him recite the **är** words on Chart 15.

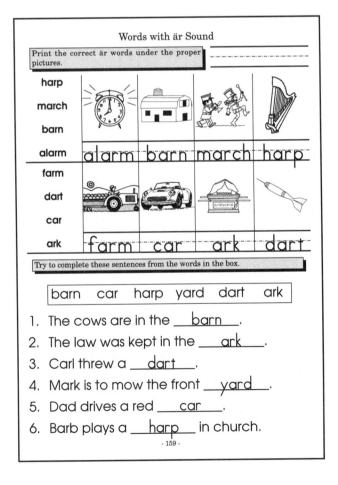

Page 160

Purpose

To give further review of **är** and **ow ou** sounds.

Lesson

Drill both **är** and **ow ou** flashcards. Print the following sets of vowels on the board. Ask the student to print the following words in the correct columns, as you dictate:

är	ow	ou
shark	town	house
spark	down	mouse
dark	frown	blouse

Ask the student to read the words in the lists at the left on page 160 and print the correct words under the pictures. Then have him complete the exercise at the bottom of the page.

Help him recite the **ow ou** words on Chart 14 and the **är** words on Chart 15.

Page 161

Purpose

To introduce the sound of **ôr** as in **corn**.

Lesson

Show the **ôr** flashcard and teach its sound. Ask your student to practice reading the following rhyming words:

cord	born	cork	forth
Ford	corn	fork	north
Lord	horn	stork	

Explain to your student that some **ôr** words look like long vowel **o_e** words as in **côre**. The **ôr** makes the same sound as in **côrn** and the **e** is silent.

Ask the student to read the words in the lists at the left on page 161 and print the correct words under the pictures. Then have him complete the exercise at the bottom of the page.

Help him recite the **ôr** words on Chart 17.

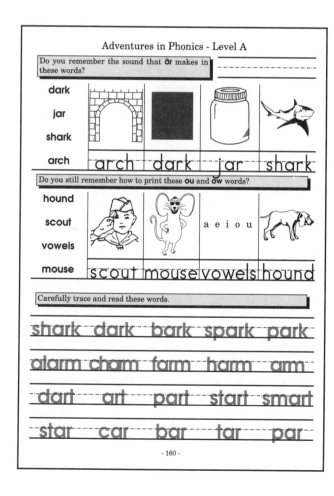

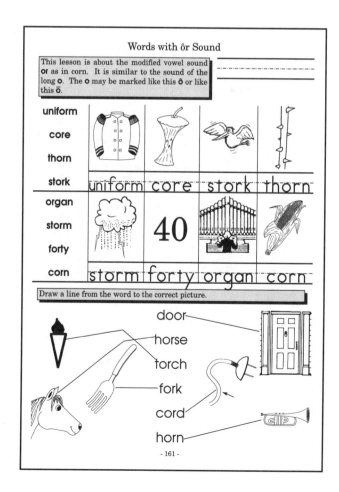

Page 162

Purpose

To review words with the sound of ôr.

Lesson

Quickly drill the three flashcards of **ow ou**, **är**, and **ôr**. Help the student to spell these **ôr** words:

ô r

horn	Lord	fort	porch	fork
born	cord	port	north	cork

Explain to your student that some **ôr** words look like long vowel **o_e** words as in stôre, shôre, and snôre. The **ôr** makes the same sound as in côrn and the **e** is silent.

Discuss page 162 and have the student recite the words before he does the written work.

Help him to read the **ôr** words on Chart 17.

Page 163

Purpose

1. To provide more review for the **ôr** sound.
2. To briefly review long vowel **a_e** words.

Lesson

Quickly drill the three flashcards **ow ou**, **är**, and **ôr**.

Have the student read these sentences:

Ten storks flew to the fort.

The fork fell to the floor by the cord.

A storm blew on the shore.

Discuss page 163 and have the student recite the words before he does the written work. For the exercise at the bottom of the page, have him circle the correct words that match the pictures.

Help him to read the **ôr** words on Chart 17.

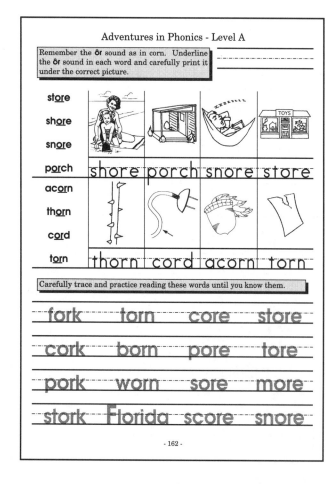

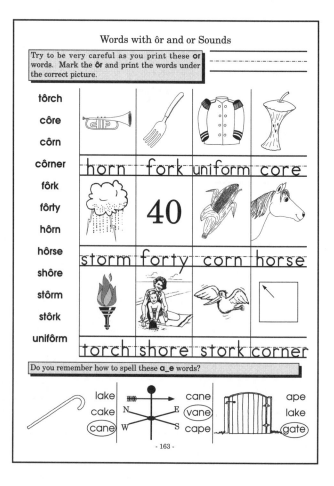

Page 164

Purpose

To give a review of words with the sounds of **är** and **ôr**.

Lesson

After reviewing their flashcards, print **är** and **ôr** on the board and ask the student to spell the following words under the correct columns, as you dictate:

ôr	är
corn	card
porch	smart
short	garden
organ	march

Read the words on page 164 before doing the work independently.

Help the student to read the **är** words on Chart 15 and the **ôr** words on Chart 17.

Page 165

Purpose

To introduce words with the sound of **ōō** as in **zoo**.

Lesson

Show the **oo** flashcard as you teach the sound, saying that it has the same sound as the long vowel **u**. Have your student read the following rhyming words several times:

goose	hoop	pool	boot	booth
loose	loop	spool	root	tooth
moose	stoop	tool	toot	

The marking of this sound is **ōō**. Explain that the **oo**, in the words above should be marked in this way.

Have the answers given orally before they are written with a pencil.

Help the student recite the **ōō** words on Chart 18.

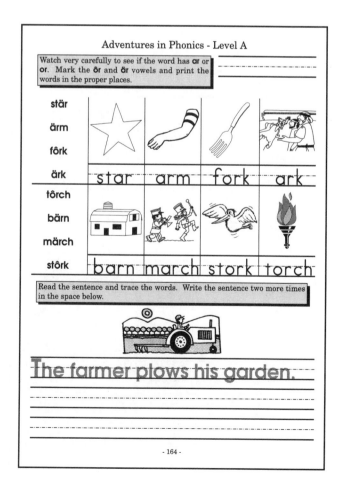

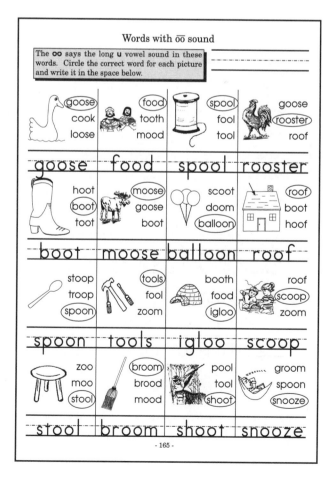

Page 166

Purpose

1. To review words with the $\overline{oo}$ sound.

2. To briefly review long vowel **i_e** words.

Lesson

Quickly drill the four flashcards for **ow ou**, **är**, **ôr**, and **oo**. Help the student print these **oo** words:

zoo	spoon	broom	tool	hoop
too	moon	groom	fool	loop

Ask the student to read the words in the lists at the left on page 166 and print the correct words under the pictures. Then have him complete the exercise at the bottom of the page.

Help the student recite the $\overline{oo}$ words on Chart 18.

Page 167

Purpose

To give further review with words that have the $\overline{oo}$ sound.

Lesson

After a quick drill of the four flashcards **ow ou**, **är**, **ôr**, and **oo**, listen as the student reads the words on page 167. For further review, look back to previous lessons that may be helpful.

Have your student complete this lesson.

How many minutes does it take to read the $\overline{oo}$ words on Chart 18?

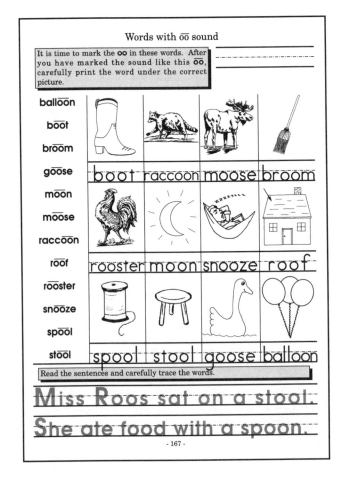

Page 168

Purpose

To introduce words with the ŏŏ making the sound as in **book**.

Lesson

Show the flashcard **oo** and teach the sound. Ask the student to read these words several times. Can he notice the difference between o̅o̅ and ŏŏ?

book look shook brook cook

hood foot good woodpecker

For page 168, have the student give the answers orally before he completes the work in pencil. For the last exercise on the page, have him circle the correct words that match the pictures.

Page 169

Purpose

To review the sound of ŏŏ, and introduce the same sound made by **u** as in **pull**, **o** as in **wolf**, and **ou** as in **would**.

Lesson

Quickly review the flashcards, giving notice to the **u** and **o** printed on the **oo** flashcard. Ask the student to read these words:

push	pull	full
puss	put	bush
wolf	wolves	
would	could	should

For page 169, have the student give the answers orally before he completes the work in pencil. Encourage neat work.

Help the student to recite the words on Chart 19.

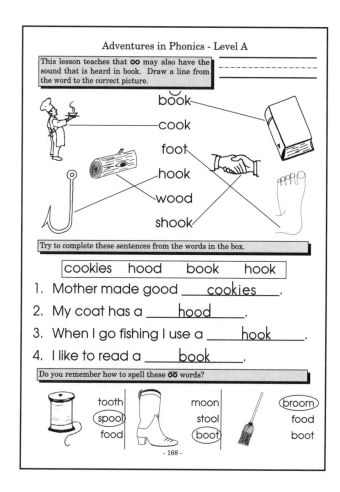

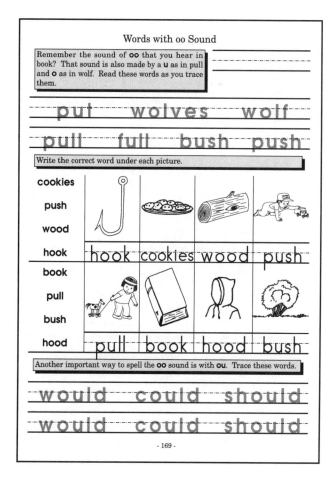

Page 170

Purpose

To review the two sounds of **oo**—long vowel **u** and ŏŏ as in **book**.

Lesson

Show the long vowel **u** flashcard, as well as the ōō and ŏŏ flashcards. Drill them many times.

Review Charts 11, 18, and 19 with the student. There are many words, so please be patient and show enthusiasm as the lesson is studied.

Carefully read all the words on page 170 before the work is completed.

Page 171

Purpose

To introduce the diphthongs **oi** and **oy**.

Lesson

Show the flashcard for **oi oy** and teach their sound. Help your student to read these words several times:

boy   boil   royalty   cowboy

oil   voice   noise   joints   coins

Quickly drill the flashcards for **ow ou**, **är**, **ôr**, ōō, ŏŏ, and **oi oy**, as well as the long and short vowels.

Ask the student to read the words in the lists at the left on page 171 and print the correct words under the pictures. Then have him complete the exercise at the bottom of the page.

Help him recite the **oi oy** words on Chart 16.

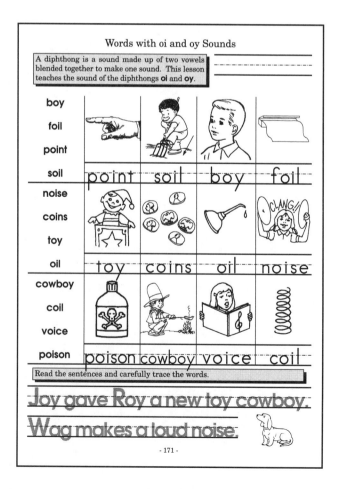

Page 172

Purpose

1. To review the diphthongs **oi** and **oy**.
2. To briefly review some short and long vowel words.

Lesson

Quickly drill the flashcards for **ow ou**, **är**, **ôr**, **o͞o**, **o͝o**, and **oi oy**, as well as the long and short vowels. Ask the student to print these **oi oy** words on the board, as you dictate them:

oi	oy
oil	toy
boil	joy
coins	boy
point	Roy

Ask that the answers be given by reading and pointing before completing in pencil.

Help him recite the **oi oy** words on Chart 16.

Page 173

Purpose

1. To give further practice in reading words with **oi** and **oy**.
2. To briefly review some short and long vowel words.

Lesson

Quickly drill the same set of flashcards mentioned in the previous lesson, giving special attention to those of which the student is uncertain.

Teach that the diphthong **oi** is usually at the beginning or middle of a word as in **oil** and **noise**. The diphthong **oy** is used at the end of a word or syllable as in **boy** and **royalty**. Discuss this rule by looking at these words and having them read:

toy   joy   Roy   royalty   loyalty   enjoy

boil   coil   foil   broil   voice   noise

Direct as the student gives answers orally for page 173. Encourage neat, independent work.

Help him recite the **oi oy** words on Chart 16.

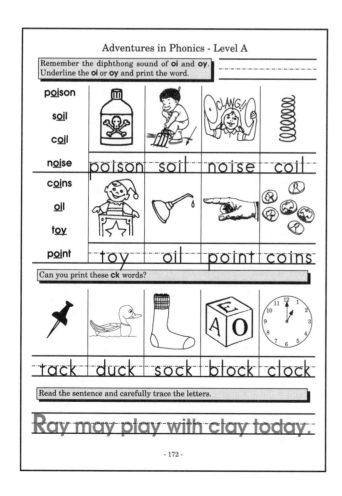

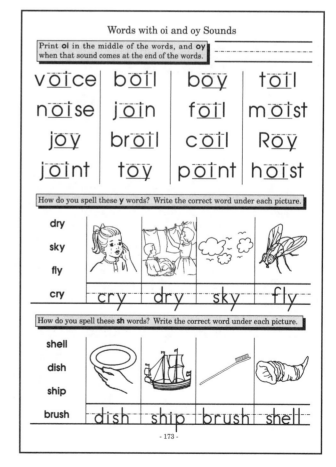

Page 174

Purpose

To introduce **er**, **ir**, and **ur** words with the sound of **ûr** as in **nurse**.

Lesson

Show the **er**, **ir**, **ur**, **ear**, and **(w)or** flashcard and give special attention to the three top sets of letters as you teach this sound. Help the student to read these words several times:

rooster	church	bird	turn	verse
spider	turkey	zipper	shirt	girl
nurse	purse	squirrel	fur	skirt
cracker	hammer	rocker	turtle	

Listen as the student reads the lists of words at the left on page 174. Have him underline the letters that make the *ûr* sound in these words. Then encourage him to print his answers on this page.

Page 175

Purpose

To give additional review of **er**, **ir**, and **ur** words with the sound of **ûr**.

Lesson

Quickly drill all the vowel flashcards, plus any consonant flashcards about which the student is still uncertain.

Before the student writes in pencil, have him read the entire page.

Help the student learn to read the lists of **er**, **ir**, and **ur** words on Chart 20.

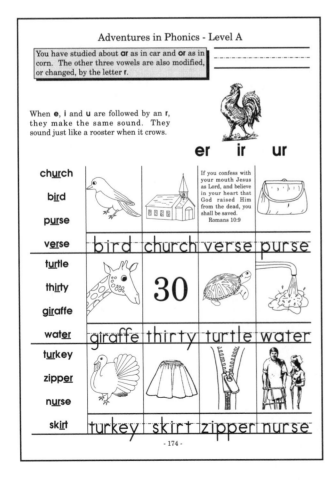

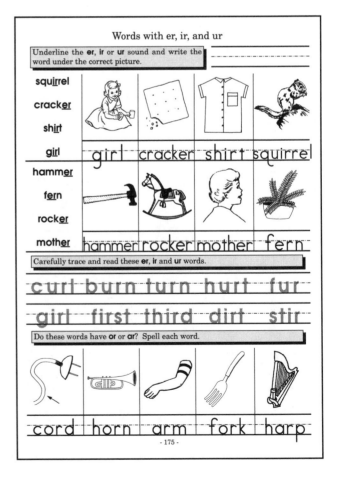

Page 176

Purpose

To introduce two more sets of letters that have the sound of ûr.

Lesson

Looking at the flashcard with **er**, **ir**, **ur**, **ear**, and **(w)or**, give special attention to the two other ways to spell the **ûr** sound—**ear** and **(w)or**.*

Have the student read these words several times:

earn   earth   early   learn   heard
word   world   work   worm   worth

Have the student answer by reading and pointing before printing.

Help the student read all the words on Chart 20.

*Note that **or** only makes this sound when it follows a **w**. That is why the **w** appears as **(w)or** in this and other lessons.

Page 177

Purpose

To review the **er**, **ir**, **ur**, **ear**, and **(w)or** words with the sounds of **ûr**.

Lesson

Quickly drill all the flashcards, giving extra attention to any that are not well known.

Listen as the student reads the **er**, **ir**, **ur**, **ear**, and **(w)or** words on Chart 20 several times or as many times as you feel necessary.

Discuss page 177 and listen to oral answers before directing them to be written.

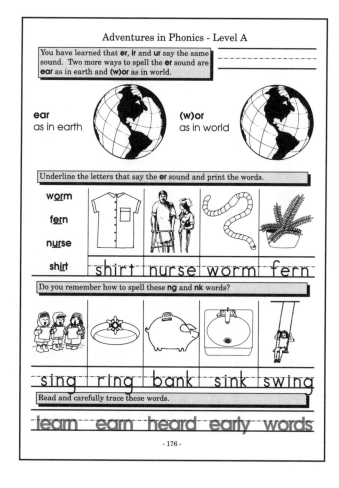

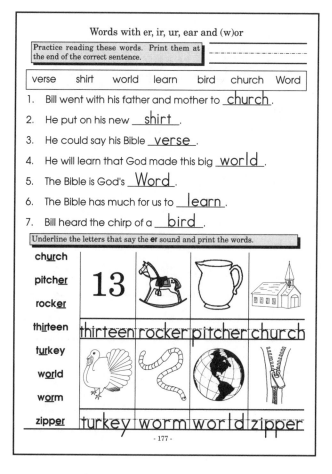

Page 178

Purpose

To teach the sound of ô as in **dog**, as well as review other sounds made by the vowel **o**.

Lesson

Looking at the flashcard for this sound, talk only about the top letter **o** as you teach the sound. Help the student to read these words:

dog	fog	log	long	song	tong
boss	cross	gloss	loss	moss	toss
moth	cloth	broth	off	soft	cost

Carefully go over page 178, having the student give the answers orally. For the exercise at the bottom of the page, he should print the correct words under the pictures. See if he can complete this lesson independently.

Listen as the student reads the first column on Chart 21.

Page 179

Purpose

To introduce the sound of ô as made by **a** when it is followed by **l**, **w**, and **u** as in **all**, **saw** and **haul**.

Lesson

Show the ô flashcard to look at all the ways this sound is made. Drill this card thoroughly, looking at the ô words below to notice the letters that make this sound:

ô	al	aw	au
dog	call	paw	haul
log	small	saw	fault
cross	tall	shawl	Paul
moth	walk	straw	Saul

In a few words, the **l** is silent when following **a** as in **walk**, **talk**, and **chalk**.

Help the student to learn the first four columns of Chart 21.

Carefully go over page 179 with the student giving the answers orally. Have him underline the letters that make the ô sound in the words in the lists at the left and print the correct words under the pictures. Then have him do the rest of the lesson.

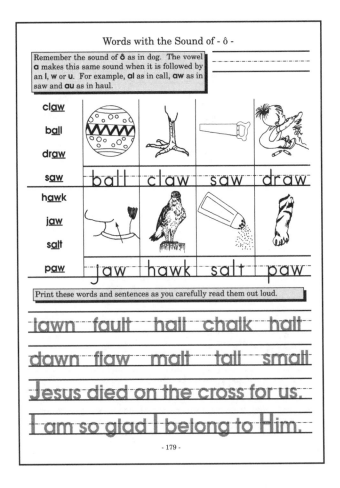

Page 180

Purpose
To review the ô sound, teaching that the letters **augh** and **ough** also make this sound.

Lesson
Quickly drill the flashcards that need work, especially the sounds of **ow ou**, **är**, **ôr**, **ōō**, **ŏŏ**, **ûr**, and **ô**.

Give special attention to the last two sounds (**augh** and **ough**) which have a silent g̶h̶. Have the student read these words many times:

| daughter | caught | taught | naughty |
| bought | brought | thought | fought |

Listen as the student reads the words on Chart 21.

Thoroughly go over page 180 by having the student read and point to the answers. Have him underline the letters* that make the ô sound in the words in the lists at the left and print the correct words under the pictures.

Remind your student to make narrow letters when printing the **augh** words in the first exercise.

*For the exercise at the top of the page, the student should underline all four letters (**augh**) which make the ô sound. However, he may want to underline only the letters **au** since the **gh** letters are silent.

Page 181

Purpose
To review words with the sound of ô.

Lesson
Before looking at this page, go back and review pages 178–180. Discuss the sets of letters on the ô flashcard. Practice reading the ô words on the Chart 21.

Thoroughly discuss page 181 before having the student complete the lesson.

Remind your student to make narrow letters when printing the words **daughter** and **awning** under their pictures.

Quickly drill the flashcards that need to be reviewed.

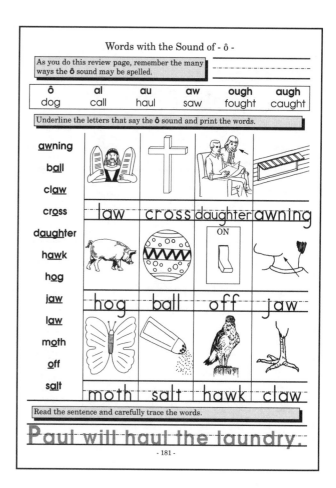

Page 182

Purpose

To review sounds from the previous lessons.

Lesson

Drill the flashcards for **ow ou**, **är**, **ôr**, $\overline{oo}$, $\breve{oo}$, and **ô**, **oi oy**, and **ûr** sounds.

Ask the student to read and underline the sounds from the flashcards in the following words that you have printed on the board:

<u>ar</u>m   t<u>oo</u>th   j<u>oy</u>   p<u>or</u>ch

d<u>augh</u>ter   b<u>oi</u>l   f<u>ough</u>t   d<u>ar</u>t

v<u>ow</u>els   gr<u>ou</u>nd   w<u>or</u>ld   <u>ou</u>t

s<u>aw</u>   <u>ear</u>th   b<u>oo</u>k   n<u>ur</u>se

Have the student read across the sound-pictures at the top of page 182 before reading the words in the list at the left.

Complete the lesson.

As pages 182–189 are studied, study one chart from numbers 14–21 each day for further review, beginning with Chart 14.

Page 183

Purpose

To continue reviewing words.

Lesson

Have the student read across the sound-pictures at the top of page 183 before reading the words in the list at the left.

Complete the lesson.

Hear the student read the words on Chart 15.

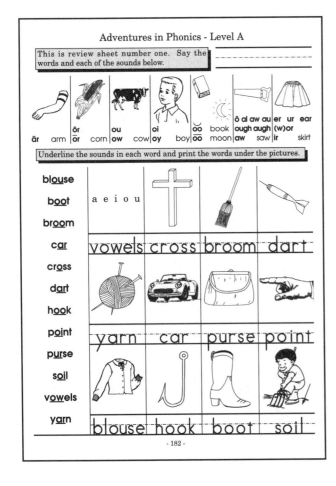

Page 184

Purpose

To have further review of reading words.

Lesson

Have the student read across the sound-pictures at the top of page 184 before reading the words in the list at the left.

Complete the lesson.

Listen as the student reads the words on Chart 16.

Page 185

Purpose

To continue review in reading words.

Lesson

Have the student read across the sound-pictures at the top of page 185 before reading the words in the list at the left.

Complete the lesson.

Hear the student read the words on Chart 17.

Page 186

Purpose

To continue review in reading words.

Lesson

Have the student read across the sound-pictures at the top of page 186 before reading the words in the list at the left.

Complete the lesson.

Remind your student to make narrow letters when printing the longer words under the pictures.

Listen to the student read the words on Chart 18.

Page 187

Purpose

To give practice in spelling words with the help of the main sound.

Lesson

If the student has understood previous lessons, a minimum of review drill will be needed. Print these sounds as headings on the board or lined paper and dictate the following words to be spelled under the correct columns:

är	ow	o͞o	ir (ûr)	ôr
barn	how	soon	bird	corn
star	now	zoo	girl	horn
harm	town	broom	shirt	horse

Point out that many words ending with an **s** sound have a silent **e** after the **s**, as in the word **horse**.

Listen as the student reads the words on Chart 20.

Go over the page to be sure the student knows all the pictures. Have him print the correct words under the pictures.

Give as little help as possible. Remember to commend or gently correct.

Page 188

Purpose

To continue to give practice in spelling words with the help of the main sound.

Lesson

Print these sound headings on the board and dictate the words to be spelled, or have the student read the lists below:

oi	ou	all	(w)or	o
join	ground	call	world	cloth
coil	pound	small	worm	dog
foil	out	fall	work	moth

Check to be sure that the student knows the pictures.

Listen as the student reads the words on Chart 21. Your student may enjoy placing a star or a special mark above the charts that he is able to read quickly.

Have your student print the correct words under the pictures to complete this lesson.

Page 189

Purpose

To give a final review in spelling words.

Lesson

Print these sounds as headings on the board and ask the student to print the words that you dictate:

oi	aw	o͝o	ôr	ûr
soil	draw	took	north	church
toil	law	cook	torn	turn
coin	hawk	shook	organ	curl

Go over the page to be sure the student knows all the pictures and have him print the correct words under these pictures.

Remind him that many words ending with the **s** sound have a silent **e** after it.

Listen to the student read the words on Chart 19.

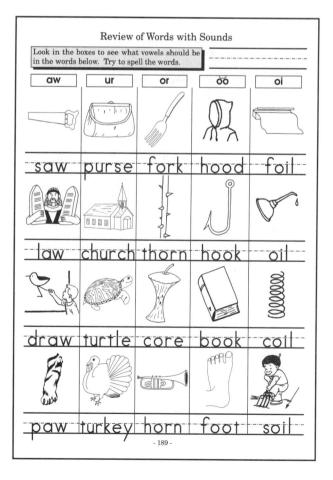

Page 190

Purpose
To introduce the sound of **âr** as in **square**.

Lesson
Quickly review the previous flashcards of **ow ou, är, ôr, ûr, oi oy, ô, o͞o** and **o͝o**. Show the new flash-card **âr** and say the groups of sounds several times, looking at the top of page 190 at the same time. Help the student read these **âr** words:

are	arr	air	err
care	carrot	air	berry
dare	carry	chair	cherry
hare	marry	fair	ferry
rare		hair	Jerry
square	ar	pair	merry
stare	Mary	stairs	Terry

ear	ere
pear	there
tear	where
wear	

After discussing the top row of âr sound-pictures on page 190, have your student give the answers orally before the work is completed in pencil.

Begin to study Chart 22 as page 190-193 are studied.

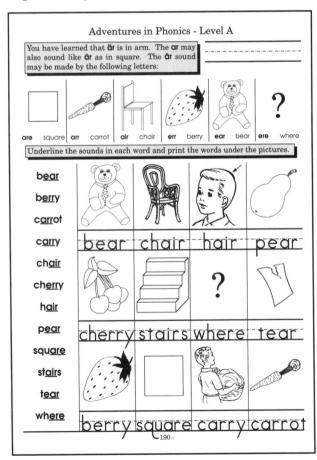

Page 191

Purpose
To review words with the sound of **âr**.

Lesson
Quickly drill with the flashcards used in the previous lesson. Have the student read the chart with **âr** words.

After discussing the top row of âr sound-pictures on page 191, have the answers given orally before the work is completed in pencil.

Listen to the student read the words on Chart 22.

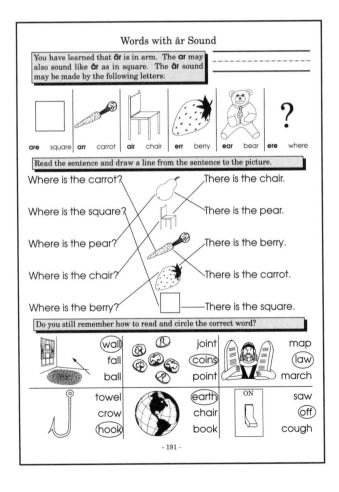

Page 192

Purpose

To continue to review words with the sound of **âr**.

Lesson

Have your student read the **âr** words on Chart 22.

After discussing the top row of âr sound-pictures on page 192, have the answers given orally before the work is completed in pencil.

Page 193

Purpose

To give further review reading words spelled with the **âr** sound.

Lesson

Have the student read the chart for **âr**. Place these letters on the board to discuss the three sounds made by **ear**:

ear (ēar)	ear (ûr)	ear (âr)
ear	early	bear
dear	earn	pear
tear	earth	tear

Did the student notice the two ways to pronounce **tear**?

Complete page 193.

Listen to the student read the words on Chart 22.

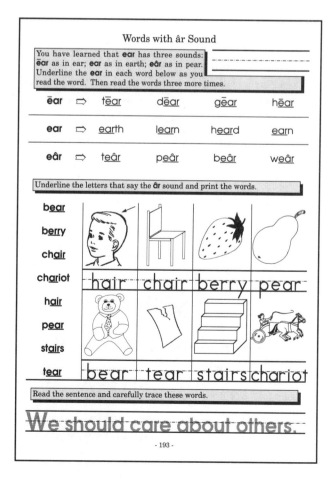

Page 194

Purpose

To introduce the rule for the hard and soft sounds of **c**.

Lesson

Explain that the consonant **c** can make two sounds.

When the vowels **a**, **o**, or **u** come after the **c**, the **c** usually has the "hard" sound of **k** as in **cat**.*

When the vowels **e**, **i**, or **y** come after the **c**, the **c** usually has the "soft" sound of **s** as in **ice**.

Help the student to read these words:

c = k sound		c = s sound	
cat	cot	Ice	circus
cob	cute	mice	city
come	cube	face	cyclone
cone	candy	circle	cymbal

Help in reading the soft **c** words on Chart 23.

Thoroughly go over page 194, then have your student read the words in the lists at the left before writing the correct words under the pictures.

*Note that the **c** also makes the "hard" sound of **k** when followed by a consonant.

Page 195

Purpose

1. To review the short and long vowel sound of **a**.
2. To examine the need for **k** instead of **c** in words such as **lake** and **cake**.

Lesson

Show the flashcard for the long vowel sound of **a** and have the words on Chart 7 read.

Make sure the student knows all the pictures on page 195.

Ask why the **k** is needed instead of the **c** in words such as **lake** and **cake**. Explain that the words would be pronounced **lase** and **case** if the **c** was printed instead of **k**. Remind him that the silent **e** makes the **c** have the soft sound of **s**.

Complete page 195.

Ask the student to do his very best printing.

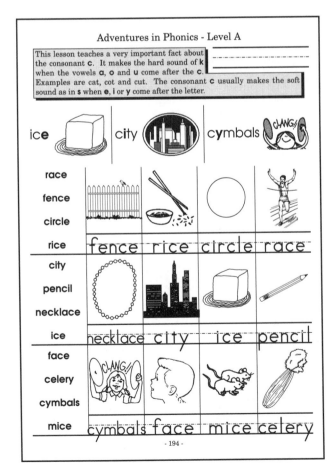

Page 196

Purpose

To introduce the rule for the hard and soft sounds of **g**.

Lesson

Explain that the consonant **g**, like the **c**, can also make two sounds.

When the vowels **a**, **o**, or **u** come after the **g**, the **g** usually has the "hard" sound of **g** as in **goat**.*

When the vowels **e**, **i**, or **y** come after the **g**, the **g** usually has the "soft" sound of **j** as in **cage**.

Help the student to read these words:

g = g sound		g = j sound	
gas	got	cage	giraffe
game	gum	page	ginger
gate	gun	pledge	gym
goat	guppy	giant	Gypsy

Some exceptions include: **girl**, **get**, **gift**, and **give**.

Discuss page 196 thoroughly before your student prints the answers.

Help him read the soft **g** words on Chart 23.

---

*Note that the **g** also makes the "hard" sound of **g** when followed by a consonant.

Page 197

Purpose

To review the short and long sounds of the vowel **i**, as well as words with the soft sound of **g**.

Lesson

Show and discuss the long vowel **i** flashcard. Have the student read the words on Chart 9, with long vowel **i**, and Chart 23, with the soft sound of **g**.

Discuss page 197 thoroughly, before the student prints the answers. For the first two exercises, he should write the correct words under the pictures. Then have him do the rest of the page.

Give your child compliments and gentle corrections as necessary.

Adventures in Phonics - Level A

Just as the **c** makes the sound of **s** when **e**, **i** or **y** comes after it, the **g** usually makes a soft sound of **j** when **e**, **i** or **y** follows it. For example, cage, gym and giant. Underline the **e**, **i** or **y** that makes the **g** have the soft sound of **j**. Read these words three times before you print them in the spaces.

badge
bridge
engine
gem
giraffe
hinge
large
pledge

badge   pledge   engine   gem

?
small

hinge   large   bridge   giraffe

From the list of words above, read and complete the sentences.

1. Bruce has a big train ___engine___.
2. At the zoo we saw a large ___giraffe___.
3. Dad drove our car on a ___bridge___.
4. The door has a black ___hinge___.
5. All policemen must wear a ___badge___.
6. Do not forget to say the ___pledge___.
7. A diamond is a very nice ___gem___.

- 196 -

Review of the Sounds of - i - and Soft - g -

Do you remember the long and short sounds of **i**? The words in this first part are spelled **i_e**.

dive   fire   bite   prize   vine

dime   five   kite   bike   hive

These words make the **g** have the sound of **j**.

bridge
giraffe
engine
hinge

giraffe   engine   hinge   bridge

Circle the correct long vowel **y** word which matches each picture.

cry   sky   cry
dry   shy   dry
fly   fry   sky

- 197 -

Page 198

Purpose

To teach how to pronounce words that have consonant digraphs **kn** and **wr**.

Lesson

Drill the flashcards for **sh, ch, wh,** and **th**. Explain
that a consonant digraph has two consonants that
make one sound. Show the **kn** and **wr** flashcards,
teaching these two rules:

The **k** is silent when followed by **n** as in **knot**.

The **w** is silent when followed by **r** as in **write**.

Help your student to read the list of words beginning with **kn** and **wr** on the back of the Consonant
Blends Chart, which is attached to the word charts.

**Discuss page 198 before the student completes
the work independently.**

Page 199

Purpose

1. To teach that the letters **ing** may be part of a
   word or a suffix.
2. To introduce the sound of **gn**.
3. To review words with **kn** and **wr**.

Lesson

Print the letters **ing** on the board and help the student to print these words:

ing		
sing	wing	ring
king	swing	bring
sling	fling	thing
string	cling	finger

**Discuss page 199 before the answers are written.
For the exercise at the bottom of the page, the
student should underline the consonant di-
graphs** *gn*, *kn*, or *wr* **in the words at the left and
write the correct words under the pictures.**

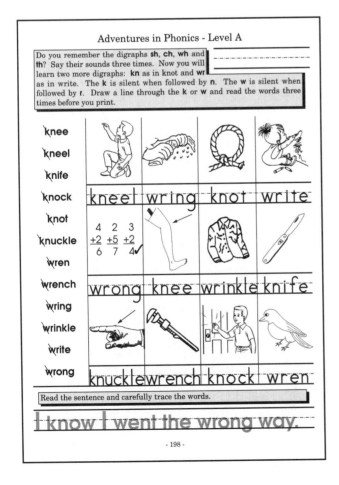

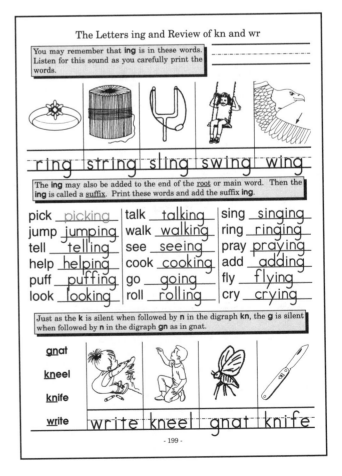

Page 200

Purpose

1. To teach the sound of **y** as a vowel at the end of words.

2. To teach that the vowel digraph **ea** says the short sound of **e** in some words.

Lesson

Discuss the following three rules for **y**:

When **y** is the only vowel and comes at the end of the word, it has the long vowel **i** sound as in **fly** and **cry**.

When **y** follows another vowel, it usually is silent as in **day** or **key**.

When a word has other vowels somewhere in it, the ending **y** has the long sound of **e** as in **baby**.

Ask the student to read these words:

by	cry	sky	why
funny	baby	happy	lady

We have learned that **ea** usually says the long vowel sound of **e** as in **bean**. However, **ea** may sometimes say short **e**. Teach your student the words on Chart 24.

Thoroughly read everything on page 200 with your student before he writes the answers.

Page 201

Purpose

To teach about the suffixes **-er** and **-y**, and review the suffix **-ing**.

Lesson

Print these words on the board and have the student read them:

call   walk   help   climb   sing   think

Add the suffix **-er** to the end of the words and have them read several times.

Print these words on the board to be read:

dust   hill   fuzz   sand   wind   sleep

Then add the suffix **-y**, explaining that it follows the rule from page 200 which said:

When a word has another vowel somewhere in it, the ending **y** has the long vowel sound of **e** as in **dusty**.

Discuss page 201 and have your student complete the exercises.

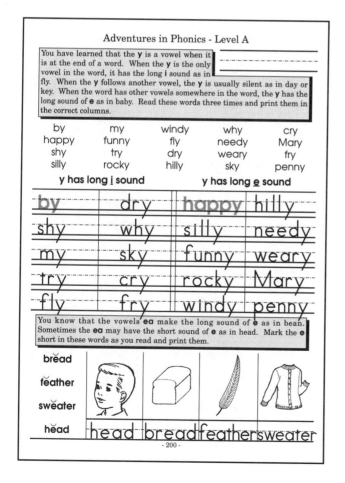

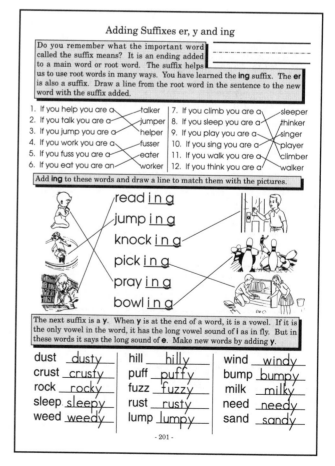

Page 202

Purpose

1. To teach that the vowel **o** may have the short vowel **u** sound as in **mother**.

2. To teach that **a** as well as all the vowels may sometimes have the short vowel **u** sound called a *schwa*, which may be printed as the symbol ∂ in a dictionary.

Lesson

Explain that **o** sometimes says the short vowel sound of **u** as in **mother**. Ask the student to read these words:

mother   love   other   smother
brother   dove   shove   glove   oven

All the vowels may sometimes make the schwa, or short vowel **u** sound. In the following words, the **a** makes the schwa sound:

a-sleep a-wake a-way a-lone

Have your student read these words, noting the various vowels and thinking about the rules.

Have the entire page read before the answers are written.

Page 203

Purpose

1. To teach about compound words.

2. To review the schwa sound of **a** and the short vowel sound **e** made by **ea**.

Lesson

Explain that two or more words may be written next to each other forming a new word. They make a bigger word which is called a *compound word*.

Print the following compound words on the board, and have your student read them. Then have him divide the words into syllables, as in **book|case**.

book|case   windmill   sailboat
earthquake pancake baseball

Listen as he practices reading the words on Chart 24.

Have your student give the answers orally on page 203, before he completes the lesson.

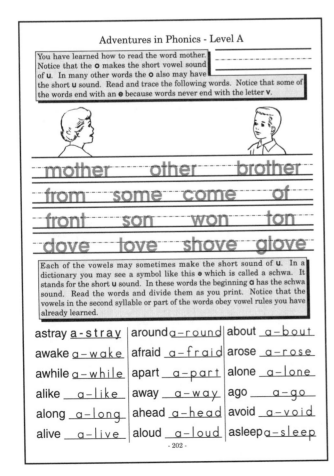

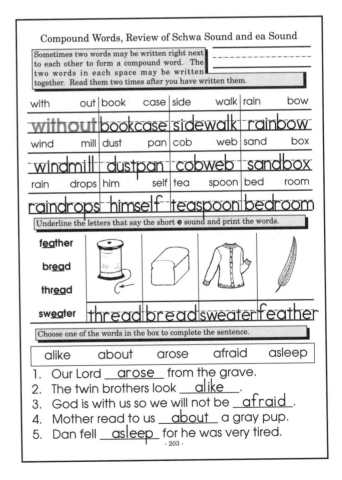

Page 204

Purpose

1. To teach words with silent letters.
2. To work with suffixes **-ing**, **-er**, **-ed**, and **-s**.
3. To review words with the sound **âr**.

Lesson

Ask the student to look at the following words and notice that each has a letter that is crossed out because it is silent:

limb   doubt   guess   build

thumb   debt   guide   built

Help him read the words, corresponding to the words above, in the last column on the back of the Consonant Blends sheet, which is attached to the word charts.

Carefully go over page 204 before having the written work completed.

Page 205

Purpose

1. To teach when indefinite articles **an** and **a** are used.
2. To review words with the **ô** sound.

Lesson

Print the following words on the board:

__ **b**all   __ **c**ar   __ **t**ree   __ **b**ook

Explain that these words begin with consonants. If we talk about only one **ball**, we would print the word **a** in front of it. Have the student print **a** on the lines provided as he reads each set of words.

Then print these words on the board:

__ **e**gg   __ **a**nt   __ **i**nch   __ **a**x

Explain that these words begin with vowels. If we talk about only one **egg**, we would print the word **an** in front of it. Have the student print **an** on the lines provided as he reads each set of words.

Reread both groups of words several times with the correct indefinite articles. These rules are helpful:

> The word **a** is used with words that begin with **consonants**.

> The word **an** is used with words that begin with **a**, **e**, **i**, **o**, or **u**.

Complete page 205. For the second exercise, print the correct words under the pictures.

Page 206

Purpose

1. To teach the rules for making words ending with **y** plural.
2. To review words with the sounds **är**, **ow**, **er (ûr)**, and **ôr**.

Lesson

Explain that the word *single* or *singular* means **one** person or thing, and the word *plural* means **more than one** person or thing:

one egg ⇨ many eggs

When working with words ending with **y**, two rules must be learned when making them plural:

1. Do not change the **y** if it is after a vowel just add **s**:

boy ⇨ boys | key ⇨ keys

2. Change the **y** to **i** and add **es** when the **y** is after a consonant:

lady ⇨ ladies | baby ⇨ babies

Review Chart 21 with the **ô** sound words.

Thoroughly discuss page 206, and have the student give the answers orally before he completes the written work.

Page 207

Purpose

To review words with silent letters and compound words.

Lesson

Teach these words, noticing the silent letters. Have them read several times:

lamb	knife	build	knot	write
hymn	knee	comb	wreath	gnaw
knock	wrap	gnat	thumb	knit
psalms	guest	doubts	wreck	walk

Review the words in the last two columns on the back of the Consonant Blends Chart, which is attached to the word charts.

Discuss page 207, and have your student recite the answers orally before he completes the written work.*

---

*Explain to your student that the word **build** in the box at the top of page 207 has a silent vowel **u**, even though the directions only say to cross out the silent consonants. This silent vowel should also be crossed out.

Adventures in Phonics - Level A

You have learned that an **s** is added to most words when more than one object is mentioned. For example egg or eggs. More than one means plural. If a word ends with **y**, two rules need to be learned. The first rule is: when the **y** follows a vowel, just add **s**.

toy s	day s	boy s	turkey s
joy s	ray s	way s	valley s
play s	key s	tray s	donkey s

The second rule is: when the **y** follows a consonant, change the **y** to **i** and add **es**. Have your teacher help you read these words three times. Do with each word as the example shows you.

lady ladies	city cities	berry berries
baby babies	sky skies	bunny bunnies
copy copies	cry cries	party parties
pony ponies	fly flies	penny pennies
story stories	lily lilies	puppy puppies

Where do these words belong? arch, crown, fern, core, dart

core | arch | crown | fern | dart

- 206 -

Review of Silent Consonants

Think again about some consonants which are silent as in these words. Print the words in the correct spaces and cross out the silent consonant.

| lamb | knife | gnat | hymn | knee |
| climb | build | knot | thumb | knock |

knot | knee | knife | gnat | lamb

build | knock | thumb | climb | hymn

Can you see the two words in these compound words? Divide the words by drawing a line between them.

rain\coat	beside	oatmeal	hayride
rowboat	beehive	pancake	sunset
necktie	into	seahorse	mailbox
baseball	cupcake	inside	himself

- 207 -

Page 208

Purpose

To review the plural form of words ending with **y**, as well as using words with **o** that have the short vowel sound of **u**.*

Lesson

Look back to page 206 and review the rules and words regarding the plural form of words ending with **y**. Asking for answers orally or in writing, test the student with these words:

toy   monkey   baby   lady   tray

turkey   copy   pony   valley   day

Listen as these words are read which have the **o** making the short vowel **u** sound:

other	mother	brother	another
love	dove	shove	glove	oven
from	some	come	front	month

Talk about the lesson before your student completes the written work.

---

*Note that the review of words with **o**, that makes the short vowel **u** sound, is only covered in the teacher's lesson, not in the workbook.

Page 209

Purpose

To review the short vowel sound of **u** that is made by the **o**, and to have extra practice in working with words spelled with the sounds of **kn** and **wr**.

Lesson

Listen again as your student reads the words with the short vowel sound of **u** made by the vowel **o** which are listed on your key for page 208.

Help him review the **kn** and **wr** words on the back of the Consonant Blends Chart, as well as all the words on page 209.

Have your student do the lesson independently.

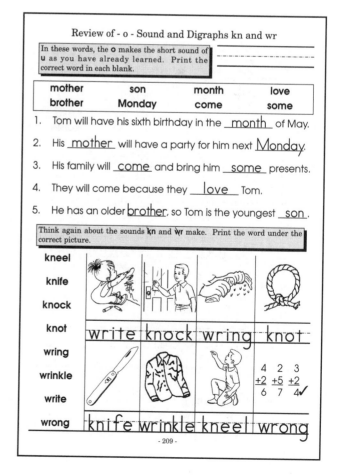

Page 210

Purpose
To review words with the soft sounds of **c** and **g**.

Lesson
Help your student read all those important words on Chart 23 until he is sure of each word.

Discuss page 210. For the first exercise, have the student read the words in the lists at the left and write the correct words under the pictures. Then have him do the exercise at the bottom of the page.

Page 211

Purpose
To review short vowel words ending with **ff**, **ll**, **ss**, and **zz**.

Lesson
Discuss these doubled consonants. Ask your student to print the following words:

ff	ll	ss	zz
cuff	chill	mess	buzz
Cliff	swell	fuss	fuzz
staff	dill	press	fizz

See how quickly he can read these words:

cuff	spell	will	dress
huff	tell	quill	press
puff	well	dull	mess
stuff	bill	gull	kiss
staff	fill	doll	miss
bell	hill	pass	fuss
fell	kill	glass	buzz

Have your student do the lesson independently.

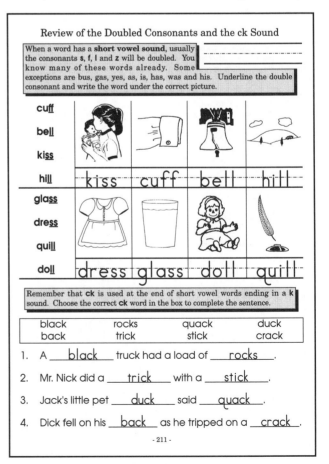

Adventures in Phonics - Level A

What happens when **e**, **i** or **y** come after a **c** or **g**?
* The letter **c** usually has the sound of **s**.
* The letter **g** usually has the sound of **j**.

pencil
city
race
circle

circle pencil race city

bridge
hinge
engine
giraffe

bridge engine hinge giraffe

gem
ice
celery
large

celery gem large ice

Print the correct word in the blank to complete the sentence.

| giraffe | pledge | mice | rice | large | cage |

1. Two little __mice__ came and ate our __rice__.
2. A __large__ crowd said the __pledge__ to the flag.
3. We saw a __giraffe__ in a large __cage__ at the zoo.

- 210 -

Review of the Doubled Consonants and the ck Sound

When a word has a **short vowel sound**, usually the consonants **s**, **f**, **l** and **z** will be doubled. You know many of these words already. Some exceptions are bus, gas, yes, as, is, has, was and his. Underline the double consonant and write the word under the correct picture.

cuff
bell
kiss
hill

kiss cuff bell hill

glass
dress
quill
doll

dress glass doll quill

Remember that **ck** is used at the end of short vowel words ending in a **k** sound. Choose the correct **ck** word in the box to complete the sentence.

| black | rocks | quack | duck |
| back | trick | stick | crack |

1. A __black__ truck had a load of __rocks__.
2. Mr. Nick did a __trick__ with a __stick__.
3. Jack's little pet __duck__ said __quack__.
4. Dick fell on his __back__ as he tripped on a __crack__.

- 211 -

Page 212

Purpose

To review the use of the indefinite articles **an** and **a**, and to have additional practice with words spelled with the sound of **o**.

Lesson

Explain again that the word **a** may be used before words beginning with consonants. Print the following exercise on the board:

__spider __tiger __cap __giraffe

Ask your students to notice that these words begin with consonants. Have him print **a** on each blank and read the exercise several times.

Next print these words on the board:

__ elephant   __ insect   __ ox   __ ant

Explain that these words begin with vowels, and that when talking about only one of each of these, we must use the word **an** before the words. Read the exercise several times:

Use **a** with words beginning with consonants.

Use **an** with words beginning with vowels.

Review Chart 21 before completing the page.

Congratulations for finishing this book!

Adventures in Phonics - Level A

An **a** is used before a word beginning with a consonant: **a** car, **a** tree, **a** lamb. The word **an** is used before a word beginning with a vowel: **an** ark, **an** elephant, **an** ant. Print **a** or **an** correctly in these sentences.

1. Sam can see __a__ bug and __an__ ant on __a__ log.

2. Mother will open __a__ door and turn on __a__ light.

3. Tom ate __an__ egg and __a__ muffin for breakfast.

4. Dad cut down __a__ tree with __an__ ax.

5. Bill hit __a__ ball with __a__ bat.

6. We saw __an__ elk and __a__ bear in the woods.

7. Have you ever seen __a__ squirrel eat __an__ apple?

Can you print these ô words?

| salt | cross | ball | hawk | frog |

Choose the correct word in the box to complete the sentence.

| laws | taught | Talk | all | daughter |

1. Mr. Hall read from the Bible to his __daughter__.

2. We ought to obey __all__ of God's __laws__.

3. Your teacher has __taught__ you many lessons.

4. __Talk__ to your teacher about your thankfulness.

- 212 -